Accounting Fundamentals

A Non-Finance Manager's Guide to Finance and Accounting

Shihan Sheriff

Table of Contents

Dedication

To my late mother, Fahima, whose love and wisdom continue to guide me, and my loving father, Azizdeen, for his unwavering belief in me.

To my incredible wife, Sheika, my rock and soulmate, and our wonderful son, Atheeq, who brings endless happiness and inspiration.

To my supportive sister, Shamikha and brother, Muhiyadeen, for their constant encouragement.

And to all my cherished and dear family, friends, and colleagues for their love, support, guidance, and faith in my abilities.

This book is dedicated to each of you, with all my love and gratitude.

Author Bio

Introducing Shihan Sheriff, a highly accomplished Chief Financial Officer at Esanjo and VP of Finance at Nomod, a Y Combinator-backed global business and technology powerhouse based in Dubai, United Arab Emirates.

Shihan's exceptional educational background features two Master of Business Administration degrees—a general MBA from Torrens University in Australia and a specialized MBA in Data Science and Artificial Intelligence from Collège de Paris, France.

He is also a qualified member of prestigious global accounting bodies such as CIMA (Chartered Institute of Management Accountants), United Kingdom; CPA Australia; CGMA (Chartered Global Management Accountants) in the US; and UAECA in the U.A.E.

Over the past few years, Shihan has completed more than 100 diverse online certification courses on various subjects, including Finance, Accounting, Data Science, Self-help, Leadership, Compliance, Statistics, Research, Business Mastery, and Process improvement, to name a few. He is currently pursuing a Doctorate in Business Administration.

With over 18 years of experience in finance and accounting, including over 11 years as a CFO, Shihan has developed expertise in a wide range of industries such as precious metals, real estate, investments, holding companies, tech startups, payment processing, e-commerce, warehousing and logistics, hotel management, general trading, agri-commodity trading, and many more.

Shihan's extensive career has provided him with invaluable opportunities to evaluate numerous businesses across various sectors. His unique experience working with publicly listed companies and family-owned businesses offers crucial insights for any reader of this book.

Shihan's journey from Assistant Accountant to Accountant, Finance Manager, CFO, and VP of Finance showcases his unwavering dependability, exceptional commitment, dedication, and ability to foster teamwork. Throughout his distinguished career, he has consistently earned promotions in recognition of his superior performance.

As a senior finance professional, Shihan's diverse experiences have established him as a leading expert in the field. His determination and optimistic attitude have propelled his success, even in the face of obstacles and challenging economic conditions.

Inspired by the wise words of the great Persian poet Jalāl ad-Dīn Muhammad Rūmī, Shihan is deeply committed to continuously improving himself first and then helping others achieve their goals. This conviction forms the foundation of his personal philosophy, fueling his tenacity and driving him forward.

Shihan invites everyone to work together to realize their ambitious dreams and transform this planet into a place where success knows no bounds! His passion for education led him to write this book, aiming to enlighten readers on the crucial areas of finance and accounting.

When not immersed in the world of finance and accounting, Shihan passionately participates in social welfare work. He has previously served as the Director Secretary and Director of Business Development for the Sri Lankan Business Council in Dubai, actively supporting the community, including the management of his own publishing company, SS Coaching, LLC, U.S.A.

In his leisure time, Shihan enjoys spending time with his lovely family and watching sports, particularly tennis and cricket, which bring excitement and camaraderie into his life.

To get in touch with Shihan, please email him at info@MoneyMasterHQ.com or send a message via the contact form on his website:

https://MoneyMasterHQ.com

Connect with Shihan on LinkedIn at

https://www.linkedin.com/in/shihan-sheriff/.

Acknowledgements

In the words of Warren Buffet, "Accounting is the language of business." It is the language that I wish to share through the book with non-finance managers, business owners, and anyone in general interested in the field of finance and accounting.

Recognizing the challenges many face in grasping complex financial concepts, I have made it a priority to present the information in an easy-to-understand and relatable manner, ensuring that readers from diverse backgrounds can benefit from this knowledge.

As the renowned author and motivational speaker Tony Robbins once said, "The only impossible journey is the one you never begin." I truly believe that anyone can learn these essential concepts and principles, and it is my sincere hope that this book ignites that flame within its readers.

With over 18 years of finance and accounting experience, including more than 11 years as a CFO, I have poured my knowledge, research skills, and passion into crafting this book with the best resources possible.

The loss of my cherished mother, grandmother, and other close relatives since 2021 has been a particularly trying time for me personally. Amidst the grief and turmoil, I found solace in my mission to make the world a better place, one informed decision at a time.

As I embarked on this journey, I was reminded of a quote by Hellen Keller: "Alone we can do so little; together we can do so much." I am immensely grateful for everyone who supported me throughout the process of writing this book–your assistance and encouragement have been invaluable. Your contributions have transformed this book from a personal dream into a shared reality.

Aside from the general appreciation, I would also like to mention a few specific names. I would like to thank: Tony Robbins, who has been a great inspiration in my life during the most difficult time, Dean Graziosi, Tony Robbins's partner, who also inspired me; Chris Haroun, who initially sparked the idea to publish my own books; Sophie Howard, a best-selling author and online entrepreneur, from whom I learned how to publish books on Amazon; and my results coach from the Tony Robbins Team, Allison Bush, who always kept me in check to achieve my goals.

To all the readers, I leave you with the inspiring words of Nelson Mandela: "Education is the most powerful weapon that you can use to change the world." By embracing the lessons within these pages, presented in an accessible and engaging manner, you are not only investing in your own success but also contributing to the collective betterment of the business world.

May this book serve as a catalyst for positive change and a foundation for a brighter future.

Shihan Sheriff

ACMA, CGMA, MBA (General), MBA (Data Science & AI),
CPA (Australia), UAECA (UAE)

Introduction:

Unveiling the World of Finance for Non-Finance Managers

Proper accounting is like engineering. You need a margin of safety. Thank God we don't design bridges and airplanes the way we do accounting. –Charlie Munger

Because accounting and finance are fields where numbers, spreadsheets, and financial jargon rule, they may seem inaccessible to those without a formal education in the subject. However, hidden behind the complex web of financial statements and cash flow assessments is a powerful tool that can be used to gain insight into company processes, make better decisions, and propel an organization to greater success.

Welcome to *Accounting Fundamentals*, a ground-breaking book carefully written by a writer who has experienced the life-changing effects of financial literacy firsthand. We will delve into an informative study of the underlying concepts and principles that drive the world of finance, simplifying complex issues, and equipping readers from a wide range of professional backgrounds with the knowledge they need to succeed.

But before we dive into the exciting world of finance, please allow me to introduce myself as your author. I am a seasoned financial expert with extensive experience and a genuine interest in bridging the knowledge gap between the financial sector and other professions. This guide grew from my never-ending quest for clarity and simplicity, as well as my unwavering commitment to the growth of individuals and organizations.

The inspiration for this book stemmed from a strong desire to demystify finances and make them approachable for those who may have previously found them intimidating. It became clear to me that there was a gap in the market for providing non-finance managers with the financial knowledge and understanding they would need to make meaningful contributions to their companies and begin the path to professional development.

In this extensive journey, we will delve into the inner workings of finance and accounting. Financial decisions are based on a set of concepts that we will investigate, ranging from the historical roots of these fields to the interaction of finance and accounting within the larger framework of the company. We will delve into the fascinating world of financial accounting principles and tenets, deconstructing their significance and emphasizing their real-world applications.

You will learn the fundamental financial terms needed for any significant financial analysis or understanding as we progress. We will thoroughly examine financial statements, including the relationship between the balance sheet, income statement, and cash flow statement, as well as the insights they may provide.

We will also do some in-depth research into business analytics and financial ratios. You will learn how to analyze financial data in a variety of ways, uncovering previously unknown connections and drawing conclusions that will guide your next steps.

This book goes beyond a cursory examination of financial concepts to serve as a reference for real-world business situations. We will define key accounting terms, deconstruct the complexities of tax compliance, and shed light on the importance of break-even analysis and budgeting.

Furthermore, we will look at management accounting and its importance in making strategic decisions and measuring performance. We will untangle the complexities of determining how profitable a new investment will be, deciding between debt and equity funding, and sketching a road map for your company's future based on what we learn.

I have included chapter quizzes and summaries after each section to ensure you get the most out of this educational journey. As you continue reading, you will gain the knowledge, understanding, and confidence needed to successfully navigate the financial world and benefit from its potential for increased personal and professional development.

Buckle up, readers, because we are about to embark on an adventure that will change your life as we explore the exciting world of finance through the eyes of managers who work in fields other than finance. Prepare to learn the language of numbers and use it to solve puzzles, reveal secrets, and uncover untapped potential. Let us embark on a journey to educate, inspire, and liberate your inner financial whiz.

How to Use This Book

Accounting Fundamentals: A Non Finance Manager's Guide to Finance and Accounting is designed to be your comprehensive guide to the world of finance and accounting. The book is organized into 13 chapters, each addressing a different aspect of finance and accounting.

To maximize the benefits of this book, consider the following steps:

- **Start from the beginning:** Begin with Chapter 1, "The Importance of Finance and Accounting." Each chapter builds upon the previous one, so reading the chapters in order will provide a more coherent understanding of the concepts.

- **Take your time:** Don't rush through the material. Take time to digest and understand the concepts, terms, and principles. If necessary, re-read or go back to sections until you have a firm grasp of the ideas.

- **Familiarize yourself with the terms:** All the unfamiliar financial and accounting terms are explained in simple terms. By learning these terms, you will be able to communicate more effectively with people and colleagues in the finance world.

- **Engage with examples and quizzes:** Each chapter includes practical examples and quizzes to help you apply what you have learned and reinforce your understanding. You can check your answers to the quizzes in the resources section of MoneyMasterhq.com/Books.

- **Reflect on the chapter takeaways:** At the end of each chapter, you will find a summarizing conclusion. Use these as a quick recap of the key points discussed in the chapter.

- **Consider Chapter 13 crucial:** The final chapter, "The Business Success Blueprint Using Finance and Accounting," is particularly important. It summarizes all the previous chapters and shows you how to practically apply your newfound knowledge within your own organization.

- **Utilize online resources:** Visit MoneyMasterhq.com/Books for additional resources, including summaries, answers to the quizzes, extra content, and further explanations. These resources will further enhance your understanding and application of the concepts discussed in the book.

- **Use as a reference guide:** After your initial reading, keep this book handy as a reference guide. You can revisit specific sections or chapters as needed to refresh your memory or deepen your understanding.

- **Engage with the content:** Make notes, highlight important points, and don't hesitate to jot down any questions or thoughts that arise as you read.

This book is not just a guide—it's a tool to empower you with the knowledge and confidence to navigate the world of finance and accounting. Whether you are a non-finance manager seeking to better understand financial reports or an entrepreneur aiming to make more informed business decisions, *Accounting Fundamentals: A Non Finance Manager's Guide to Finance and Accounting* can help you succeed. Happy reading!

Chapter 1:

The Importance of Finance and

Accounting

The language of business is accounting. People often ask me what they should take in business school and/or even if they don't go to business school, what they need to know before getting into business, and I tell them, you know you have to understand Accounting. It's like being in a foreign country without knowing the language. If you're in business, if you don't understand accounting. You want to get as comfortable with that, as you are with the English language. —Warren Buffet

Welcome to the fascinating world of finance and accounting, where the numbers hide the secrets of money, investments, and corporate operations. In this chapter, we delve into the world of finance and accounting, revealing both their important obligations and their relevance.

Accounting and finance are critical to the success of any business because they serve as the foundation for making wise investments. They provide the terminology and structure for businesses to report on their financial health, evaluate potential strategies, and assess their successes and failures. Although they can be difficult to grasp at first, understanding them is essential for anyone hoping to succeed as an entrepreneur or in business.

We embarked on an adventure in the world of finance to investigate the complexities of dealing with money, investments, and risks. Budgeting, cash flow management, investment analysis, and capital allocation are just a few of the topics we will go over as we dive into the fundamentals of financial management. Individuals and businesses alike can better weather the financial markets' storms, make informed investment decisions, and aim for long-term prosperity if they understand the fundamentals of finance.

While both finance and accounting are essential to a successful business, finance is more concerned with long-term financial planning, investment analysis, and decision-making, while accounting is more focused on the immediate past and focuses on recording, summarizing, and reporting financial transactions to stakeholders. Almost as much as finance is an art form, accounting can be thought of as a science.

Finance and accounting are not only important in the business world; they also have significant implications for individuals. Personal financial planners and financial advisors play an important role in ensuring a secure financial future and making sound investment decisions. They are the economic backbone, influencing government spending and assisting in resource allocation. In this chapter, we'll delve into the crucial aspects of accounting and finance so that you'll be better equipped to handle the complex world of numbers. Let's take the first step together on this educational journey and learn how to navigate the ever-shifting financial landscape with confidence and understanding.

History of Finance and Accounting

Accounting has evolved significantly since its inception, both in terms of methods and the impact it has had on society. An early form of accounting may have emerged 12,000 years ago when people exchanged goods while subsisting primarily on hunted animals and gathered fruits.

Accounting in the modern era, on the other hand, involves a variety of technological processes and is responsible for sales amounts in the billions of dollars. According to the Business Research Company (2022), the accounting services market is expected to be worth $588 billion in 2021 and $1.7 trillion by 2031.

Throughout its history, the accounting profession has undergone significant transformations in response to societal factors such as technological advancements, economic downturns, and ethical quandaries. It is critical to understand the history of accounting in order to fully comprehend many aspects of societal change over time.

Accounting: A Historical Overview

Accounting provides businesses with accurate and up-to-date financial information to make informed decisions. It helps to track income, expenses, and cash flow, enabling decision makers to assess profitability, manage costs, and identify areas for improvement. An important part of accounting is cash flow management. By using cash inflows and outflows, we are able to identify potential cash shortages and manage working capital effectively Accounting provides financial insights, supports decision making, and ensures compliance and business growth. It serves as a guiding compass for owners to navigate the financial aspects of their business.

While the origins of accounting go back centuries, it wasn't until tax records were kept on clay tablets around 3300 B.C. that the profession was officially recognized (Miller, 2019). These artifacts were discovered in Egypt and the region formerly known as Mesopotamia. Historians believe that the Egyptians used accounting at the same time to keep track of their pharaoh's wealth and detect instances of fraud.

Accounting's Major Development Eras

Accounting has undergone significant transformations over the years, leading to the emergence of various developmental eras. While the categorization of these eras may differ depending on perspective, here are some alternative ways to classify them:

Traditional vs Modern Era

The conventional era was a time in history when accountants primarily kept records and books. Manual procedures, basic financial reports, and a focus on regulations were all hallmarks of this system.

More sophisticated methods and tools have become the norm in the modern era. Computerization, more complex financial reporting standards, and a heightened focus on analysis, interpretation, and decision-making are all part of it.

Pre-Industrial, Industrial, and Post-Industrial Revolution Era

The time before the Industrial Revolution (before the late 18th century) is considered to be the Pre-Industrial Revolution Era. In terms of formalization and standardization, accounting was fairly primitive in those days. Simple bookkeeping procedures were used to document monetary dealings.

The Industrial Revolution brought significant advancements in technology, manufacturing, and commerce. Accounting in this era witnessed the rise of double-entry bookkeeping, the development of financial reporting frameworks, and increased demands for more sophisticated accounting systems.

The Post-Industrial Revolution Era refers to the period after the mid-20th century when technology and globalization greatly impacted business practices. Accounting during this era experienced further automation, the proliferation of international accounting standards, the advent of computerized accounting systems, and an increased focus on management accounting and decision support.

Era of Compliance, Decision Support, and Strategic Management

The era of compliance emphasizes the importance of adhering to legal and regulatory requirements. Proper accounting procedures are based on three pillars: reliable financial reporting, openness, and compliance with regulations. Accounting's importance in supplying data and analysis to back up management decision-making has come into sharper focus in the decision-support era. Evaluation of performance, allocation of resources, and development of strategies all require the use of management accounting tools and techniques. Accounting in the modern era of strategic management is more proactive and strategic. Financial and non-financial data are combined to aid in decision-making and value creation.

Emergent, Pre-Analytic, Developmental, and Modern

According to IEdunote (2018), the four major eras of accounting are emergent, pre-analytic, developmental, and modern. Each of these eras has its own set of innovations and methods. Based on this classification, the first era lasted from prehistoric times until the 15th century, while the current era lasts from 1951 to the present.

Emergent

Accounting can be traced back to the earliest periods of human history. Historians have found no evidence of accounting techniques from this time period, but they hypothesize that the first bartering of commodities and services signaled the beginning of some kind of record-keeping. This lasted until 1494, when the first book detailing double-entry accounting, a method that involves debit and credit entries, was published (IEduNote, 2018).

- **Stone Age:** Ticking cave walls, mountains, and jungles to record commodities obtained and loaned

- **Primitive:** Noting inscriptions on walls and constructing rope knots for transactions

- **Barter:** Recording agricultural or other sorts of barter arrangements

- **Currency:** Tracking European bank loan-financed monetary transactions

Pre-analytic

The pre-analytic period in accounting history is defined as the time period between 1495 and 1799 (Maryville University, 2022). Several foundational accounting concepts were developed during this time period:

- **Going concern:** A business's ability to stay open

- **Periodic inventory:** Recording financial transactions at the end of each accounting period

- **Money measurement:** Only transactions with monetary value are recorded

Development

Accountants worked during the "development" or "explanatory" period between 1800 and 1950 (Maryville University, 2022). During this time period, two major changes occurred in the business world: the introduction of joint-stock companies, which allowed many business shareholders to participate, and the Industrial Revolution, which shifted the economy of much of the world toward a manufacturing-based economy. These and other transitions during the development period led to the following outcomes:

- **Industrial Revolution:** Tracking massive amounts of capital needed to start new firms and railroads

- **Joint-stock companies:** Complicated business due to shareholders' and partners' financial concerns

- **Government regulation:** Developed uniform accounting methods to satisfy tax legislation

Modern

Accounting practices have been steadily evolving to conform to international standards since 1951, when the modern accounting era began. In response to the growing need for long-term financial forecasting, there has been a desire for accounting techniques that reliably reflect current financial conditions and reliably predict future conditions.

Accounting firms in the United States adopted GAAP (Generally Accepted Accounting Principles) to comply with regulations requiring transparent financial reporting. When preparing annual reports and quarterly financial statements, all publicly traded corporations in the

United States must adhere to these guidelines. During this time period, the following major international economic challenges influenced accounting innovations (Maryville University, 2022):

- **The 1929 stock market disaster:** Established the SEC and required accounting standards.

- **Ethics investigations:** Following high-profile cases of illicit accounting techniques by criminal Al Capone and energy corporation Enron, helped alter the profession's norms and monitoring.

Acceptance of Accounting as a Profession

The field finally gained official recognition when the first professional accounting associations were formed. Scotland was home to the first two accounting societies: the Institute of Accountants and Actuaries in Glasgow in 1854 and the Edinburgh Society of Accountants in 1855. Members of the Glasgow group called themselves "chartered accountants," and they petitioned Queen Victoria for their own charter, allowing them to practice accounting independently of solicitors.

Following that, in 1887, the AAPA was renamed the American Association of Public Accountants. In 1896, the first group of accountants took the exam that would certify them as "certified public accountants" (CPAs). The American Institute of Certified Public Accountants (AICPA) was founded in 1957 as the organization in charge of awarding the CPA designation.

A Historical Overview of Financial Accounting

Financial accounting, as a subset of accounting, is concerned with keeping track of, summarizing, and reporting financial activities relevant to a company's operations over a specific time period. Professional accountants use financial statements like these to track certain transactions:

- The balance sheet displays assets, liabilities, and shareholder equity.

- The income statement summarizes the income, expenses, gains, and losses.

- The cash flow statement depicts a company's cash flow.

Earlier Types of Financial Accounting

The use of tokens and some form of bookkeeping can be traced back thousands of years in financial accounting history, but it was not until 1458 that Benedetto Cotrugli invented the double-entry accounting system, laying the groundwork for what we now know as modern accounting. He was born in what is now the Republic of Ragusa and worked as a merchant, economist, scientist, and diplomat.

However, Luca Bartolomeo de Pacioli, an Italian mathematician and Franciscan friar, is widely regarded as the founding father of modern accounting. His book, *The Collected Knowledge of Arithmetic, Geometry, Proportion, and Proportionality*, was published in 1494 and contains a 27-page section on bookkeeping. It explains how Venetian businesspeople used two accounting methods, namely the single-entry and double-entry systems. For the first time, plus and minus indicators were used in the book.

Assets, liabilities, capital, revenue, and expenses would all be recorded in the same way that they are in modern income statements and balance sheets under de Pacioli's proposed accounting system. He took this responsibility very seriously and advised not going to bed until all of one's debits and credits had been settled.

Advances in Financial Accounting Technology

Professionals in a variety of fields have developed methods to streamline bookkeeping as a result of the tools and technology that have significantly altered financial accounting. The following are some examples of financial accounting-related developments:

Calculator

The calculator, invented by American scientist William Burroughs in the 1880s, was one of the first developments in financial accounting instruments. Instead of using tokens, clay balls, or abaci, accountants could now do their calculations more quickly and precisely with this device.

Spreadsheet Software

With its release in 1978, VisiCalc pioneered the use of computers for financial modeling using spreadsheets. In the same year, Peachtree introduced its PC accounting program. In addition to these innovations, the widespread use of QuickBooks for routine bookkeeping in 1998 simplified financial accounting.

Methods of Accounting Today

Early on in the development of accounting, a method called traditional accounting—also known as British accounting—was widely utilized. Accounting as it is practiced in the United States now provides a deeper dive into a company's financials, or "modern" accounting. Some of the benefits of staying on top of financial management are:

- data access

- trend analysis

- accurate forecasts

- competitive edge

Today, most wealthy countries use cutting-edge accounting techniques, which frequently involve the use of technology for increased efficiency and precision.

Accounting in Both Old and New Fashioned Styles

The two major accounting schools of thought employ distinctly different sets of categories and methods. The following are some key differences between traditional bookkeeping and electronic accounting systems:

Classical Accounting

There are three main types of accounting records used in standard practice. Accounts that are "personal" are those that pertain to a single individual or company, whereas "impersonal" accounts, like real and nominal ones, are those that don't apply to anyone in particular. The terms are explained below:

- **Personal:** Transactions involving an individual, business, or organization.

- **Real:** Accounts whose balances transfer over from one period of accounting to the next.

- **Nominal:** Accounts whose balances are carried over to the next accounting period with a zero balance.

Modern Accounting

The following are some of the additional ways that modern accounting classifies financial data:

- **Assets:** Valuable items owned by a corporation

- **Liabilities:** External debts

- **Capital:** The difference between assets and liabilities

- **Expenses:** Amount spent on revenue-generating objects or activities

- **Revenue:** Money a company makes by its main operations (e.g. by selling goods or providing a service)

- **Withdrawals:** The business owner takes money out for personal use.

Accounting in the Age of Technology

A variety of technical tools help accounting in the modern era record a wide range of transactions. Modern accounting tools have made it possible for accountants to devote more time to analyzing patterns and giving advice that shapes business strategies. These strategies and resources are increasingly common in contemporary accounting:

- **Digital payments:** Through the use of computers, we can now analyze and share our financial data with one another in real time.

- **Online backups:** Accounting records are stored off-site so that multiple people within an organization have access to them.

- **AI and machine learning:** Accurately and quickly evaluating vast amounts of data.

- **Blockchain:** Helps keep a ledger and securely transfer asset ownership.

Accounting vs Finance

Finance and accounting are two of the most prominent fields in the business and financial worlds. Although the terms are sometimes used interchangeably, they each serve a distinct purpose and are linked to the goal of financial literacy and success.

Finance, a dynamic field that deals with the management of funds, investments, and risks, takes a broad view. It examines how money is spent and saved in order to provide the best results and return on investment. Finance includes financial planning, cash allocation, risk management, and investment analysis. It entails the ability to analyze financial markets, make sound investment decisions, and plan for long-term success.

Accounting, on the other hand, uses methodical and thorough systems when reporting financial information. It records, processes, and interprets monetary activity in order to provide trustworthy and understandable financial reporting. Accounting is the study and practice of organizing a company's books, producing reliable financial statements, and adhering to applicable laws and guidelines. Accounting, analyzing financial statements, auditing, and legally paying taxes are all concepts covered. Financial statements are the "language of business," as they inform investors, creditors, and other interested parties about an organization's financial health.

Although finance and accounting appear unrelated at first glance, there are numerous connections between the two. Accounting information is used in finance to assess a company's financial health, make investment decisions, and forecast cash flows. Accounting, in turn, relies on financial concepts and principles to produce reliable and useful financial reports.

Individuals and businesses that want to be financially successful should learn the intricacies of finance and accounting. It provides decision-makers with the background information and practical skills they need to make sound judgments, make efficient use of available resources, and succeed in today's complex financial management environment.

Accounting and Finance as an Integral Part of the Overall Business

Finance and accounting are at the heart of any business, permeating every aspect of the operation. They have an impact on the entire organization, not just the finance department.

Financial considerations are important in two areas: strategy and resource allocation. It collaborates with other divisions to develop spending plans, research potential investments, and assess the economic viability of projects. Finance ensures that resources are used effectively to achieve organizational goals by taking into account the monetary consequences of potential actions. It enables the company to make informed decisions and pursue long-term growth by providing information on available financing sources, cost-cutting strategies, and profitability analysis.

Accounting is more than just keeping track of financial transactions. It governs the organization at all levels, recording financial transactions across all divisions, and then making sense of the data. Accounting, operations, sales, and purchasing are all responsible for accurate financial reporting. It aids in evaluating the efficiency of various departments, identifying problem areas, and ensuring adherence to rules and regulations. Accounting also supports managerial decision-making by providing critical data for assessing profitability, examining financial patterns, and making educated strategic decisions.

Finance and accounting are powerful success drivers, and companies that recognize this will maximize their use of them. By sharing information and cooperating, the finance and accounting teams can better understand the financial implications of their decisions and work to align the company's goals. Integrating these systems helps lay the groundwork for transparency, accountability, and long-term success in the financial sector.

The Double-Entry Bookkeeping System

The double-entry bookkeeping method is the accounting industry's backbone and the standard against which all others are measured. Each financial transaction has an equal and opposite impact on two accounts in the double-entry accounting system. In a double-entry system, the following equation is used to determine how each entry should be made:

$$Assets = Liabilities + Equity$$

In this method, debits always balance out credits in the general ledger, also known as the "T-account." That is, for every "credit" entry in one account, a "debit" entry exists in another.

Please keep in mind that the term "T-accounts" refers to a double-entry bookkeeping system. This method of accounting entails drawing a large letter T on the page and entering the account information above the T's horizontal line. The debits are represented on the left side of the T, while the credits are represented on the right.

Example 1.1:

ABC Corporation receives $1,000 in cash from a customer for goods sold. The cash account would be debited for $1,000. On the same day, ABC Corporation paid $500 in cash for office supplies.

The T-account for the Cash account would look like this:

Cash

Debit	Credit
$1,000	$500

The T-account provides a visual representation of the account's balance and the flow of debits and credits.

Debit and Credit

In bookkeeping, the term "debit" refers to an entry made on the left side of an account, indicating an increase in assets or expenses or a decrease in liabilities, equity, or revenue. Debits are recorded in the general ledger to accurately track the flow of financial transactions.

When a debit is made to an asset account, it means that the value of the asset is increasing. For example, if a company purchases inventory, the inventory account is debited to reflect the increase in its value. Likewise, when a company invests in new machinery or acquires assets, a debit entry is made to the asset account, indicating an increase in the value of the asset.

Debits are also used to track the expenses that a company incurs. For instance, when a business has bills to settle, such as rent or utility bills, these expenses are posted as debits in the respective expense accounts.

Liabilities are reduced when they are repaid or settled. This also results in a debit entry to the liability account (i.e., a reduction in a liability is a debit).

In certain situations, a debit can be used to decrease equity. For example, when a company distributes dividends to its shareholders, the retained earnings account (which is part of equity) is debited, reducing the overall equity.

On the other hand, the term "credit" refers to an entry made on the right side of an account. It represents an increase in liabilities, equity, or revenue, or a decrease in assets or expenses. Credits are also recorded in the general ledger to accurately track the flow of financial transactions.

When a liability account is credited, it means that the amount owed by the business has increased. For instance, if a company borrows money from a bank, the loan account is credited to reflect the increased liability for the amounts owed to the bank.

Credits are used to record contributions made by owners or shareholders to the business. For example, when an owner invests additional capital in the company, the equity account is credited to reflect the increased ownership stake.

Credits are also used to record the revenues and income generated by the business. For instance, when a company makes a sale, the sales revenue account is credited to reflect the increased total revenue.

When an asset account is credited, it means that the value of the asset is decreasing. For example, if a company sells inventory, the inventory account is credited to reflect the decrease in its value.

Additionally, credits are used to record reductions in expenses. For example, if a company receives a discount on a utility bill, it reduces the expense and, therefore, the respective expense account is credited to reflect the decrease in the company's expenses.

It is essential to note that the use of debits and credits follows specific rules and principles based on the type of account involved. Understanding these rules is crucial for accurately recording and analyzing financial transactions in bookkeeping.

The Double Entry System's Many Benefits

Here are the key benefits of using the double-entry accounting system:

- **Enhanced accuracy and error detection:** If a debit or credit entry is mistakenly recorded, the imbalance between the debits and credits becomes apparent when reviewing the accounts or preparing financial statements. This prompts accountants to investigate and correct errors quickly.

- **Comprehensive financial information:** By examining the balances of various accounts and their relationships, managers can identify trends, assess financial performance, and make informed decisions. The double-entry system allows for the calculation of financial ratios, comparisons between different periods, and evaluation of profitability, liquidity, and solvency measures.

- **Facilitates financial reporting and analysis:** The double-entry system provides a solid foundation for financial analysis and decision-making. It enables the calculation of financial ratios, such as profitability ratios, liquidity ratios, and leverage ratios, which help assess the company's financial health and performance.

- **Improved accountability and transparency:** The double-entry system encourages the division of duties within an organization. Different individuals or departments are responsible for different stages of the accounting process, such as recording transactions, preparing financial statements, and reconciling accounts. This separation of duties helps prevent collusion and reduces the risk of fraud. It improves accountability by ensuring that multiple individuals are involved in the accounting process, providing checks and balances.

- **Compatibility with GAAP and IFRS:** This entry system is designed to comply with accounting standards and regulations. It provides a structured framework for recording financial transactions and preparing financial statements in accordance with Generally Accepted Accounting Principles (GAAP) or International Financial Reporting Standards (IFRS). Compliance with these standards ensures transparency and accountability in financial reporting, allowing stakeholders to understand and evaluate the financial position and performance of the organization.

The Double Entry System: A Practical Guide

This is the golden rule of double-entry bookkeeping, so remember it. In a perfect world, debits and credits would cancel each other out.

- When employing a double-entry method to keep track of money flows, debits go to the left and credits go to the right in the general ledger.

- The debit column is where assets and expenses go, whereas the credit column is where liabilities, revenue and equity are recorded.

- Assets = Liabilities + Equity and the total of all Debits balance out the total of all Credit balances in the end.

Account Types in the Double-Entry Accounting System

The double-entry system is based on several different types of accounting records. Let's go over them quickly:

Asset Account

Debit entries increase an asset account's balance, while credit entries decrease it. Cash, real estate, and vehicles are all examples of assets.

Liability Account

A company's liability accounts are where it keeps track of its debts to third parties. Debiting a liability account lowers the company's liability, whereas crediting the account raises the company's current liabilities. Amounts owed to suppliers, bank loans, and taxes payable to the government are all examples of liabilities.

Income or Gains Account

The income or gains of a company are recorded in the income or gains accounts. Income can also be divided into two subcategories: gains and revenues. Here, the company records any income it has received. Sales are a great example of an income account. Interest income and service fees are two other examples.

Equity Account

A company's equity account is where it records the monetary value of its shareholders' equity. Examples of equity are share capital, accumulated earnings of the business (retained earnings), and reserves.

Expenses Account

In its expense reports, the company keeps track of money that leaves or will leave the company. Outgoing financial commitments include salary, utilities, rent, and insurance.

A Double-Entry System in Action

As an example, consider the purchase of office supplies. This is a double-entry system for documenting the purchase of office equipment:

Particulars	Debit	Credit
Office Supplies	$40,000	
Cash		$40,000

You can see that the same transaction has resulted in debit and credit entries for two different accounts. Let's look at a different scenario to better understand. Let's use rent expense payments as an example this time:

Particulars	Debit	Credit
Rent Expense	$60,000	
Cash		$60,000

In this scenario, by paying rent expenses in cash, the cash in the business has been reduced. That is a reduction in an asset. From what we explained earlier, the reduction of an asset is a "credit," and hence, cash is a credit.

On the other hand, we have paid our rent expense, i.e., an increase in expenses. From what we discussed earlier, we learned that an increase in an expense is a debit. As such, we debit the rent expense.

Why Is Finance and Accounting So Important?

Accounting and finance departments are critical to the continued existence, growth, and prosperity of all successful businesses. Financial performance can be measured, analyzed, and improved with their assistance, making these departments critical.

Businesses cannot ignore the impact of economic realities unless they have access to accurate financial data. You can use the knowledge and skills you gain to make sound financial decisions, prioritize your spending, and plan for the future. Strong financial management results in the ability to successfully manage risks, identify profitable investment opportunities, and comprehend the complexities of the financial markets. If company leaders do not understand financial concepts, the company faces financial instability and missed growth opportunities.

Why? Because accurate accounting ensures the credibility of reported financial data, it protects the interests of those with a vested interest in an organization by making truthful information about that entity's financial standing available. Businesses that follow Generally Accepted Accounting Principles (GAAP) can demonstrate regulatory compliance, gain the trust of investors, and make well-informed strategic decisions based on timely financial data. Without proper accounting procedures, businesses risk non-compliance, financial irregularities, and even legal and reputational consequences.

Finance and accounting work together to establish the terminology and framework within which a company can communicate its financial story. They facilitate long-term success by allowing executives at all levels to take calculated risks and think strategically. Information obtained through good financial and accounting practices can assist businesses in anticipating risks, seizing opportunities, and adapting to ever-changing market conditions.

Finance and accounting are critical components of a successful business because they assist people in making sense of the complex world of assets, investments, and financial transactions. Finance and accounting are powerful tools that can assist businesses in making sound decisions, gaining the trust of their investors, and setting themselves up for long-term success.

Quiz

1. **Why is understanding accounting and finance crucial for individuals and businesses?**

   (A) It helps with decision-making.

   (B) It aids in budgeting and financial planning.

   (C) It facilitates effective resource allocation.

   (D) All of the above

2. **Which of the following best describes the relationship between accounting and finance?**

   (A) Accounting is a subset of finance.

   (B) Finance is a subset of accounting.

   (C) Accounting and finance are interchangeable terms.

   (D) Accounting and finance are distinct but closely related disciplines.

3. What is the primary purpose of the double-entry system of accounting?

(A) To ensure accurate record-keeping

(B) To maintain the balance of the accounting equation

(C) To facilitate error detection

(D) All of the above

4. In the context of business, which of the following is a key difference between accounting and finance?

(A) Accounting focuses on recording and reporting financial transactions, while finance focuses on the management of financial resources.

(B) Accounting deals with investments, while finance deals with taxes.

(C) Accounting is concerned with long-term financial planning, while finance focuses on short-term financial management.

(D) Accounting primarily deals with external stakeholders, while finance deals with internal stakeholders.

5. Which of the following is an advantage of the double-entry system of accounting?

(A) Simplified record-keeping

(B) Enhanced accuracy and error detection

(C) Reduced need for financial statements

(D) None of the above

6. **Which of the following innovations have significantly influenced modern accounting practices?**

(A) The invention of the printing press

(B) The development of computerized accounting software

(C) The introduction of cryptocurrencies

(D) The establishment of the stock market

7. **In the double-entry system of accounting, what does a debit entry represent?**

(A) An increase in assets or expenses

(B) A decrease in liabilities, equity, or revenues

(C) Both A and B

(D) None of the above

For the answers to this and the other quizzes, visit
MoneyMasterHQ.com/Books.

Chapter Takeaway

This chapter provided a foundational understanding of accounting by introducing its historical roots, distinguishing it from finance, introducing the concept of the double-entry bookkeeping system, and discussing the various accounts that make up this system.

We have seen how accounting has a long history, stretching back thousands of years, and how it is adapted over time to meet the demands of various industries and cultures. The evolution of contemporary accounting methods can be better understood in light of this background knowledge. Furthermore, we learned that accounting and finance are two separate but related fields. Accounting offers a common language and set of tools for doing this, while finance is concerned with the management of money, investments, and financial markets.

We also examined the double-entry bookkeeping system, which requires every transaction to have equal debits and credits, balancing the equation, and thereby ensuring accuracy, error detection, thorough financial information, and openness. Assets, liabilities, equity, revenues, and expenses are the five main types of accounts used in the double-entry accounting system. Different kinds of accounts are used for different purposes in accounting, allowing businesses to evaluate their financial standing and make smart choices based on accurate data.

In order to interpret financial information, work effectively with finance professionals, and make educated business decisions, non-financial managers need an understanding of the history, principles, and significance of accounting. Managers can aid in their company's short and long-term financial health and growth by recognizing the significance of finance and accounting.

Segue to the Next Chapter

The following chapter delves deeper into the core ideas upon which financial accounting is built. Understanding the assumptions and principles upon which financial accounting is based is essential to gaining a firm grasp on the subject. Read on to learn them!

Chapter 2:

Basic Financial Accounting

Concepts and Assumptions

We begin our study of the foundational principles upon which the field of financial accounting is built. The goal of these explanations is to help you better understand the concepts underlying financial reporting.

Financial accounting communicates a company's financial status to all stakeholders in a language they can understand. In order to ensure consistency and comparability across organizations and industries, it employs a standardized framework. The principles and assumptions of financial accounting are what make this possible, as they specify how monetary information should be presented.

The cornerstone of financial accounting is made up of basic accounting principles. These principles provide a theoretical basis for understanding and making use of accounting rules. Accuracy, reliability, significance, and comparisons all fall under this heading. Financial accountants use these guidelines to ensure their clients receive useful, accurate data.

In addition to the ideas themselves, financial accounting is based on assumptions. All accounting theory and practice are based on these underlying assumptions. The entity assumption, which states that the company is a separate legal entity from its owners; the ongoing business assumption, which states that the company will continue to operate indefinitely; and the unit of money assumption, which states that every financial transaction is recorded in the same unit of currency, are all critical assumptions.

Everyone, from sole proprietors to institutional investors, must understand the fundamentals of financial accounting. They provide a framework for comprehending a company's financial records, assessing its health, and making confident decisions based on consistent metrics.

The following chapters will go over each of these introductory ideas and premises in greater detail. We'll get into what this means, how it may be used in practice, and why it's important for accurate financial reporting. Join me on this exciting adventure as we explore the foundational concepts and assumptions of financial accounting that influence our global economy.

The Accounting Principles

The organizational structure and operational practices of a company are reflected in key accounting assumptions. They serve as a framework for recording financial and business transactions. If any of the above-mentioned assumptions prove to be incorrect, a company's financial statements may need to be revised.

Accounting concepts underpin GAAP (Generally Accepted Accounting Principles), and all GAAP concepts and regulations are derived from fundamental accounting principles. Traditional accounting practices are the source of some accounting principles, while the Financial Accounting Standards Board (FASB) is responsible for others.

It will be beneficial to have a firm grasp on these fundamental concepts as you study accounting. This is not like studying for an accounting exam and then forgetting everything two days later. These concepts will appear throughout your accounting textbooks.

Accounting Basics: What Are They?

The GAAP consists of various standards for financial reporting including the below:

Conservatism Principle

When there are competing theories about how to record a transaction, accountants should err on the side of caution and record expenses and debts as soon as practically possible. In the same spirit, they only write down income and profits when they happen. This accounting theory encourages conservatism, so if your accountant employs it, they are more likely to anticipate losses rather than profits or revenues in the financial statements. Remember, this theory can only be applied when the accountant has more than one reasonable option for recording the transaction. Even if an accountant wants to err on the side of caution, they cannot ignore all other accounting principles.

Full Disclosure Principle

According to this rule, anything that could "materially affect" a user's choice regarding the company should be included in the financial statements' footnotes. By being transparent about their accounting practices and potential outcomes, this company has eliminated any potential for future fraud. The basic idea behind this principle is that the business owner or accountant should always be provided with complete and correct information regarding the company's financial transactions.

Cost Principle

According to the cost-benefit principle, if it takes too much time and resources to compile and report financial data, then those activities should be cut. So, if recording something unimportant is going to cost the company a lot of money, it shouldn't be done. The lesson for business owners to take away from the fundamental rule of accounting is to never equate price with worth. Assets depreciate or appreciate in value over time, but you won't see a change in value unless you sell the asset or record the depreciation. You should hire an appraiser instead of depending on the financial records if you require a reliable appraisal of your company that doesn't involve selling off assets.

Going Concern Principle

The premises underlying the going concern concept, also known as the "non-death principle," are that the business in question will continue to exist and carry out its operations beyond a particular point in time. In other words, the going concern principle holds that the company will not go out of business in the near term.

This has several implications that affect financial statement reliability, decision making, continuity of operations, auditing, and assurance:

- **The going concern principle ensures the accuracy of financial statements by requiring that they be prepared under normal business conditions.** The financial statements are more indicative of the company's actual assets, liabilities, and equity because of the assumption of business continuity. This improves the trustworthiness of the financial data presented to various parties, such as shareholders, lenders, and investors.

- **The going concern principle is an important guiding principle for any decision that needs to be made.** The continuity of operations is assumed, allowing management, investors, and other stakeholders to make future plans with confidence. This assumption is fundamental when contemplating potential investments, developing expansion plans, and calculating the company's long-term financial health.

- **Maintaining business as usual is crucial, which is why the going concern principle stresses this point.** It motivates top-level executives to think about the company's future viability, profitability, and financial stability. The company's continued success and growth are dependent on the management team's willingness to treat it as a "going concern," rather than a "going out of business" sale.

- **When it comes to auditing and providing assurance, the going concern principle has far-reaching implications.** Financial statements are analyzed and conclusions about the company's viability as a going concern are drawn. Auditors may issue a qualified opinion or highlight a matter in the audit report if they have concerns about the company's ability to continue operations. This serves as a warning to those who have a vested interest in the company's future success that there are many factors that could go wrong.

Matching Principle

All expenses, regardless of when they were paid, must be recorded alongside related revenues in the same period in which they were incurred. Together, this concept and the principle of revenue recognition are responsible for ensuring that all income and expenses are reported on an accrual basis. Compensation of employees, commissions on sales, certain fixed overhead, and the like are all examples of such costs. However, your accountant might still use the accrual foundation of accounting, even if you file your taxes using the cash method. It is more beneficial to analyze your company's performance and profitability using accrual-based reports because they adhere to the matching principle and are more accurate than cash-based statements.

(Please refer Accrual Based Accounting and Cash Based Accounting on Pages 154 and 155)

Revenue Recognition Principle

The revenue recognition principle is an accounting principle that provides guidelines for determining when and how to recognize revenue in financial statements. It outlines the criteria for recognizing revenue from the sale of goods, rendering services, or other business activities. This principle ensures that sales-related income is properly recorded at the time it is earned, rather than waiting until payment is received. Using this fundamental accounting concept, a company can report a monthly profit even though it hasn't received any cash during that period.

Specific Time Period Assumption

To adhere to the specific time period assumption, a company's financial statements must cover a single, clear time period. Another condition of this concept is that the date range being considered for analysis be clearly stated within the financial statement itself. This idea explains why your financial statements (balance sheet and income statement) always show information as of a certain date and for a certain time period.

Materiality Principle

This theory shows how important it is for an accountant to be informed and meticulous. Since the size of businesses varies, an item that is important to one may not be important to another. It is the accountant's duty to decide what is important and what may be ignored. When balancing records, if an accountant finds a mistake or a difference, they may decide that it doesn't matter much. In such a case, it is up to the accountant's judgment to decide whether or not the sum in question is negligible.

Economic Entity Assumption

The economic entity assumption treats a business as a separate entity from its owners. It maintains its own records, financial statements, and distinct financial activities. This principle ensures transparency and accuracy in reporting, aiding stakeholders, and assessing the entity's financial performance and position. Therefore, it matters most that the transactions correctly reflect the activity of the company. Based on the economic entity assumption, an individual who is analyzing a company's records believes that all of the transactions related to the company are being reviewed.

Monetary Unit Assumption

According to the principle of the monetary unit assumption, all monetary transactions must be documented in the same currency. This is the rationale behind why you need to keep proper records of your company's international financial dealings. The stability of a currency's purchasing power is another key assumption behind this accounting principle. That is to say, even though a company has been around for decades, it will not consider inflation when reporting its financials.

Quiz

1. Which of these helps with financial data recording, reporting, and analysis?

(A) Financial statements

(B) Accounting principles

(C) Financial ratios

(D) Cash flows

2. Where do accounting principles fit into the bigger picture?

(A) Making sure that financial statements are consistent and easy to compare

(B) Figuring out how profitable a company is

(C) Managing cash flows well

(D) Doing financial research

3. Name the principle or assumption that treats a business as a separate entity from its owners.

(A) Matching principle

(B) Economic entity assumption

(C) Going concern principle

(D) Revenue recognition principle

4. When it comes to accounting, the time period concept means:

(A) That the company will be around forever

(B) That the reporting period for financial statements should be finite

(C) That all transactions should be recorded in the local currency

(D) That assets and liabilities should be valued using historical costs

5. Which of the following assumptions is based on the notion that business transactions must be reported in the currency of the country in which the company operates?

(A) Monetary unit assumption

(B) Time period assumption

(C) Historical cost assumption

(D) Going concern assumption

6. The accrual method of accounting records revenue and expenses when they are earned or incurred, regardless of when the associated cash flows occur.

(A) True

(B) False

For the answers to this and the other quizzes, visit
http://MoneyMasterhq.com/Books.

Chapter Takeaway

In this chapter, we delved into the fundamental concepts that serve as the foundation for financial accounting. We also learned how to use generally accepted accounting principles to record, report, and understand financial data. These standards ensure that the financial statements of various organizations can be compared in a reliable manner.

In addition, we looked at accounting assumptions, which are fundamental concepts that form the foundation of financial accounting. Time period assumptions, monetary unit assumptions, going concern assumptions, and past cost assumptions all influence how financial data is measured and reported.

Understanding these concepts and presumptions is critical for evaluating financial statements and applying accounting principles successfully. They provide a standardized framework for recording and reporting a company's financial health, performance, and cash flows.

Segue to the Next Chapter

The following chapter, "Basic Financial Terms," expands on the concepts presented here by providing an overview of the most basic principles in finance and accounting. In this lesson, I will define some of the most common terms used when talking about financial statements, ratios, and analysis. With the knowledge gained in this chapter, you will be able to analyze and comprehend financial data with confidence!

Chapter 3:

Basic Financial Terms

Whether you are just starting out in the field or want to improve your own financial literacy, learning some basic financial jargon is a good idea. You will be better equipped with this knowledge, whether you are managing your personal finances or speaking with a tax accountant or another financial professional. If you have this information, you will be able to better communicate your ideas to coworkers, customers, and investors.

Understanding the complexities of the financial sector begins with learning the terms used. It assists you in understanding financial statements and projections, evaluating investment opportunities, and weighing the outcomes of your decisions. Understanding financial terms like "revenue," "expenses," "assets," and "liabilities" will help you evaluate a company's financial health, identify risks, and seize opportunities.

Furthermore, understanding these concepts promotes productive teamwork and dialogue in the workplace. It enables you to have fruitful discussions about money with coworkers, ensuring that everyone is on the same page. Your ability to use financial jargon confidently and professionally will increase your credibility with clients and investors.

By learning a broader range of financial terms, you can finally take control of your financial future and master the nuances of the financial world. Investing in yourself in this way will pay off in the long run with better financial knowledge, wiser decisions, and more satisfying work connections. Learning and mastering these words is essential, whether you are starting a career in finance or simply trying to get a better handle on your personal finances.

Financial Terms: Why Are They Important?

Working knowledge of financial terminology is a must for everyone who wants to take charge of their own financial future or the future of a company. To better prepare for meetings with investors and accountants, for example, it is helpful to have this background knowledge. When applying for a loan, renting or purchasing a home, and saving for retirement, financial literacy comes in handy. Another advantage is keeping up with the latest economic news and developments.

Knowing these terms could help your career and productivity at work, depending on your field. For instance, if you have a job in finance, accounting, sales, or another sector that is somewhat comparable, you can use various financial phrases on a regular basis in order to carry out your responsibilities and communicate effectively with coworkers and customers. Similarly, whether you're in charge of the finances of your organization, drafting financial statements, or doing bookkeeping, you'll need a firm grasp of these words.

Revenue

Earnings from selling goods or rendering services are known as revenue. It's the lifeblood of a company—the money that pays the salaries and rent.

Example 3.1:

XYZ Retail sells 100 smartphones at a price of $500 each during a particular month. The company's revenue is the number of smartphones sold multiplied by the price per smartphone. In this example, the company's revenue is $50,000. Revenue represents the total amount of money earned from the sales made.

Expenses

The costs of running a business are known as operating expenses. Rent, payroll, utilities, and anything else essential to running a firm are all examples of operating costs.

Example 3.2:

ABC Services provides cleaning services. One of their big expenses is the cost of cleaning supplies. The company purchases cleaning supplies like detergents, disinfectants, mops, and vacuum cleaners in the course of their business. Each month, ABC Services spends $500 on cleaning supplies to ensure that they have adequate stock for their cleaning operations. This $500 expense is recorded in their financial statements as a cost of doing business.

The cost of sales refers to the direct expenses incurred by a company to produce or buy the goods it sells. It represents the costs directly associated with the production or procurement of the products or services that generate revenue for the company.

Example 3.3:

Company XYZ Electronics manufactures and sells electronic devices. They produce smartphones and incur various costs in the process, like raw materials, direct labor, and manufacturing overhead expenses. During the year, XYZ Electronics purchased $500,000 worth of raw materials, incurred $200,000 in direct labor costs, and had $100,000 in manufacturing overhead expenses.

Cost of sales

= cost of raw materials + direct labor cost + manufacturing overhead expenses

= $500,000 + $200,000 + $100,000

= $800,000

In this case, XYZ Electronics' cost of sales for the whole year was $800,000. The cost of sales is an important part of a company's income statement. The gross profit is calculated by taking the company's revenue and subtracting the cost of sales. The gross profit represents the amount of revenue left after deducting the cost of goods sold and directly associated expenses.

Gross Profit

Gross Profit is a measure that indicates how much money a company makes from its core business operations after deducting the direct costs associated with producing/delivering its products/services. It is calculated by subtracting the cost of sales from the revenue. GP reflects the profitability of the company before considering other expenses (like overhead costs and/or taxes). It gives an idea of how efficiently a company is generating revenue from its products or services and is often used as an indicator of the company's initial profitability.

Example 3.4:

In our example of ABC Cleaning Services, the company's gross profit will be all the money received from clients to whom it provides a service less any costs directly associated with providing such services.

Gross Profit = Revenue - Cost of Sales

Other Income

"Other income" refers to the money a company makes from sources aside from its main business. Capital gains, interest from investments, and rents collected are all forms of passive income.

Example 3.5:

ABC Suppliers has a shop downtown. Customers use their parking lot during the week, but on Sundays, when the store is closed, they rent it out to a driving school, which uses it for their clients to practice parking. The rental income received from the driving school falls under "other income."

List of Major Expenses

The term "major expenses" refers to significant or substantial costs incurred by a company or an individual that have a notable impact on their financial well-being. Major expenses are typically significant in terms of their monetary value or impact on the overall budget or financial statements.

Employee salaries, rent or lease payments for business premises, raw materials or inventory purchases, marketing expenses, and equipment or machinery purchases are all examples of major expenses for businesses. These expenses frequently consume a sizable portion of the company's resources and have a direct impact on its financial performance.

It is critical for both businesses and individuals to identify and manage major expenses in order to maintain financial stability and make sound financial decisions. Budgeting, cost-cutting measures, and strategic planning can all help reduce the impact of major expenses and ensure financial sustainability.

Example 3.6:

Let's look at the major expenses ABC Manufacturing may incur:

- **Raw materials:** ABC manufacturing purchases raw materials, like metals, plastics, or chemicals, to manufacture its products. The cost of raw materials can be a significant expense for the company, especially if it requires bulk quantities or specialized materials.

- **Labor costs:** Employee salaries and benefits are a major expense for most companies. ABC Manufacturing employs a significant workforce, including production workers, engineers, and administrative staff, which incurs ongoing payroll expenses.

- **Utilities:** Running a manufacturing facility requires utilities such as electricity, water, and gas. The consumption of these utilities can result in substantial expenses for ABC Manufacturing.

- **Rent or mortgage payments:** If ABC Manufacturing operates its production facility in a rented space or owns a building through a mortgage, the associated rental or mortgage payments would be considered a major expense.

- **Research and development:** ABC Manufacturing invests in research and development to improve existing products and develop new ones. The cost incurred in research activities, prototyping, and testing can be significant.

- **Marketing and advertising:** Marketing efforts such as advertising campaigns, trade show participation, and online marketing are required to promote products and reach target customers. These activities incur costs that help ABC Manufacturing gain visibility and grow.

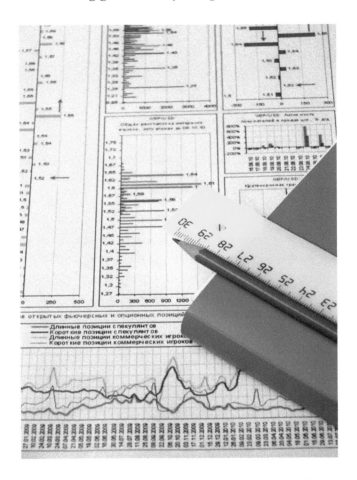

EBITDA

Earnings before interest, tax, depreciation, and amortization are abbreviated as EBITDA. It's just a fancy way of saying a company's profit before deducting things like interest, taxes, and asset depreciation.

Example 3.7:

Let's look at ABC Manufacturing, which produces and sells custom-made furniture. Their EBITDA will look as follows (Tamplin, 2023b):

- **Revenue:** ABC Manufacturing generates $1,000,000 in revenue from the sale of their furniture

- **Operating expenses:** ABC Manufacturing has operating expenses of $200,000

- **Interest:** ABC Manufacturing pays $30,000 in interest on loans it took to finance its operations.

- **Taxes:** ABC Manufacturing incurs $20,000 in income taxes based on its taxable income.

- **Depreciation and amortization:** ABC Manufacturing has $50,000 worth of depreciation expenses due to the wear and tear on its machinery and equipment.

- **Amortization:** ABC Manufacturing does not have any intangible assets to amortize.

To calculate EBITDA (Earnings Before Interest, Taxes, Depreciation, and Amortization), calculate the Operating Income:

Operating income
$$= \text{Total revenue - cost of sales - operating expenses}$$
$$= \$1,000,000 - \$500,000 - \$200,000$$
$$= \$300,000$$

Add back the depreciation and amortization

EBITDA
$$= \text{operating income + depreciation and amortization}$$
$$= \$300,000 + \$50,000$$
$$= \$350,000$$

This means that ABC Manufacturing made $350,000 from its core operations before taking into account interest payments, taxes, and depreciation expenses. EBITDA provides a measure of the company's ability to generate income solely from its operations without considering certain financial factors.

Other Comprehensive Income (OCI)

The term "Other Comprehensive Income (OCI)" is used to describe any profits or losses that are not included in the net income of the company. It represents changes in equity that occur from transactions or events that are not part of regular business operations. These items are usually reported in the comprehensive income statement, which is an extended version of the income statement.

Example 3.8:

Let's look at the OCI for a company called XYZ Corporation. In a particular accounting period, XYZ Corporation reports the following items:

- **Net income:** XYZ Corporation earned a net income of $500,000 during the period. This is the traditional measure of profit and loss derived from its regular business operations.

- **Unrealized gain on available-for-sale securities:** XYZ Corporation had investments in the stock market. During the period, the value of these investments increased by $100,000, but the company did not sell them. This unrealized gain is considered part of other comprehensive income.

- **Foreign currency translation adjustments:** XYZ Corporation has subsidiaries operating in different countries. Fluctuations in exchange rates can impact the value of these subsidiaries' financial statements when translated into the reporting currency. In this period, there was a translation of

$50,000 due to favorable exchange rate movements. This gain is also included in other comprehensive income.

In this example, XYZ Corporation's net income is $500,000, which represents its profit from regular business activities. However, the company also has other comprehensive income due to the unrealized gain on available-for-sale securities and the foreign currency translation adjustments.

The total comprehensive income

= net income + other comprehensive income

= $500,000 + ($100,000 + $50,000)

= $650,000

OCI provides a more comprehensive view of a company's financial performance by including gains and losses that may not have an immediate impact on cash flow or net income. It reflects changes in equity as a result of particular occurrences or transactions that are not routine business operations but may still have an impact on the company's overall financial position.

Depreciation and Amortization

Depreciation

Depreciation is the process by which a business records the wear and tear that causes its physical assets to lose value over their useful lives. It is commonly used for assets like buildings, vehicles, machinery, and equipment. Depreciation recognizes that these assets gradually wear out or become less valuable over time due to factors like age and wear and tear.

Example 3.9:

XYZ Manufacturing owns a delivery truck. The truck is expected to have a useful life of 10 years. The useful life refers to the estimated duration over which an asset is expected to be productive and generate economic benefits for a business. The company purchased it for $50,000. Instead of expensing the entire cost upfront, XYZ Manufacturing can spread the cost of the truck over its useful life by applying depreciation. If they choose to use the straight-line method (one of the methods used to calculate depreciation), they can allocate $5,000 ($50,000 divided by 10 years) as an annual depreciation expense. This helps XYZ Manufacturing account for the gradual decrease in the truck's value over time.

Amortization

Where depreciation works with physical or tangible assets, amortization works with intangible assets over their useful lives. These assets include things like patents, copyrights, trademarks, and licenses. Amortization realizes that these assets only provide value to a company for a specific period, and their cost should be spread out accordingly.

Example 3.10:

XYZ Manufacturing acquired a patent for a new technology. The patent costs $100,000 and has a useful life of 20 years. To account for the cost of the patent, XYZ Manufacturing can use amortization. If they choose to amortize the patent using the straight-line method, they would allocate $5,000 ($100,000 divided by 20 years) as an annual amortization expense. This helps XYZ Manufacturing recognize the gradual consumption of the patent's value over its useful life.

Net Profit

When revenue is subtracted from costs, taxes, and interest, the remaining amount is known as net profit. This is the money left over after a business has paid its expenses. It is the bottom line of the income statement and reflects the overall profitability of the business.

Example 3.11:

Let's again look at XYZ Manufacturing as an example. In a given period, the company generated $1,000,000 in total revenue from sales of its products. To calculate net profit, we need to subtract all the expenses incurred by the company during the period.

Expenses may include:

- **Cost of goods sold (COGS):** These are the direct costs involved in producing the products, like raw materials, labor, and manufacturing expenses. Let's say XYZ had COGS of $600,000.

- **Operating expenses:** These are the costs associated with the day-to-day running of the business and include things like rent, utilities, salaries, marketing, and administrative expenses. Let's assume XYZ Manufacturing had operating expenses of $200,000.

- **Interest and taxes:** These are the amounts the company pays in interest on loans and income taxes. For this example, let's say XYZ Manufacturing paid $50,000 in interest and $100,000 in taxes.

To calculate the net profit, we subtract the expenses from the total revenue.

Net Profit

= Total revenue - (COGS + operating expenses + interest + taxes)

= $1,000,000 + ($600,000 + $200,000 + $50,000 + $100,000)

= $50,000

The net profit is an important indicator of how much money the company has earned from operations after covering all costs. In this way, investors, lenders, and business owners can easily assess the financial health and profitability of a company.

If the resultant number was negative, we call it a net loss, meaning the company has lost money instead of making money.

Retained Earnings

The term "retained earnings" refers to profits that a company does not distribute to shareholders. They function as the business equivalent of a savings account, from which funds for expansion, debt repayment, or emergencies can be drawn as needed.

Example 3.12:

XYZ Manufacturing has been in operation for several years and has accumulated profits from its business activities. Let's say the company's net profit for the current year is $100,000.

To calculate the retained earnings, we need to consider the opening balance of retained earnings from the previous year and add the current year's net profit while subtracting any dividends paid to shareholders.

Let's assume that XYZ Manufacturing had a beginning retained earnings balance of $300,000, paid $20,000 in dividends to shareholders, and recorded a net profit of $100,000 for the current year.

Retained earnings

= opening balance of retained earnings + net profit - dividends

= $300,000 + $100,000 - $20,000

= $380,000

In this example, XYZ Manufacturing's retained earnings for the current year would be $380,000. This represents the portion of the company's net profit that has been retained and added to the cumulative total of retained earnings. Retained earnings are an important way to fund growth, debt repayments, and investments internally. By investing its profits, the business shows commitment to future growth and sustainability.

Dividend Payouts

Dividend payouts refer to the distribution of a company's profits to its shareholders as a return on their investment (ROI). When a company earns a profit, it has the option to distribute a portion of that profit to its shareholders in the form of dividends.

Example 3.13:

Assume that XYZ Manufacturing has generated a net profit of $500,000 for the current year, and the company's board of directors decides to distribute a dividend to its shareholders. The dividend payout is usually expressed as a certain amount per share or as a percentage of the company's earnings.

Let's say XYZ Manufacturing has 1,000,000 shares, and the board of directors decides to distribute a dividend of $0.50 per share.

To calculate the total dividend payout, we multiply the dividend per share by the number of shares:

Dividend payout

= dividend per share x number of shares

= $0.50 x 1,000,000

= $500,000

Dividend payouts provide a way for companies to share their profits with shareholders and provide them with a return on their investment

(ROI). The board of directors of the company typically decide whether to pay dividends, and this decision may change depending on the company's dividend policy, cash flow, and future growth plans. Not all companies pay dividends; some may choose to reinvest their profits for expansion or other strategic initiatives.

Assets

An asset is something that a person or business owns that has value and can be used to generate future benefits. Assets can be physical objects like buildings, vehicles, or inventory, or they can be intangible, like patents, trademarks, or even money owed to the company. Assets are typically recorded on a balance sheet, which is a financial statement that shows an entity's assets, liabilities, and equity. There are two main groups of assets: current assets and non-current assets.

Current Assets

Current assets are assets that are expected to be converted into cash or used up within a short period of time, usually within a year. These assets are considered liquid and readily available for use in the company's day-to-day operations.

Examples of current assets include:

- **Cash and cash equivalents:** This includes cash in hand, cash in bank accounts, and short-term investments that can be easily turned into cash.

- **Accounts receivable:** These are the amounts that customers owe the company for goods or services they bought on credit.

- **Inventory:** This refers to the goods or products that a business keeps on hand to sell or use in the normal course of business.

- **Prepaid expenses:** These are costs that have already been paid for, such as rent, insurance, or supplies that will be used soon.

Example 3.14:

Let's consider a company called ABC Retail, whose current assets include:

ABC Retail has $50,000 in cash in its register and $100,000 in its bank account. It also has $80,000 in outstanding invoices from customers who have purchased goods on credit. ABC Retail also has $200,000 worth of merchandise, including clothing, electronics, and accessories, ready to be sold. The company has made an advance payment of $10,000 for rent on its retail space for the next six months.

Current assets

= cash + accounts receivable + inventory + prepaid expenses

= ($50,000 + $100,000) + $80,000 + $200,000 + $10,000

= $440,000

Non-Current Assets

The assets of a corporation that cannot be quickly turned into cash over an extended period (over a year) are called non-current, or long-term, assets. These assets provide value to the company over an extended period.

Examples of non-current assets include:

- **Property, plant, and equipment:** This includes land, buildings, machinery, vehicles, and other tangible assets used in the production or operation of the business.

- **Intangible assets:** Assets that lack physical substance like patents, copyright, goodwill, and trademarks.

- **Long-term investments:** Investments made by the company in other companies or assets that are held for the long term.

Example 3.15:

ABC Retail has the following non-current assets:

ABC Retail owns a retail store building valued at $500,000, and store fixtures and equipment worth $100,000. The company also holds a trademark for its brand name, which is valued at $50,000. ABC Retail has invested $150,000 in shares of another retail company, expecting returns over five years.

Non current assets

= property + intangible assets + long term investments

= ($500,000 + $100,000) + $50,000 + $150,000

= $800,000

Total assets

= current assets + non-current assets

= $440,000 + 800,000

= $1,200,000

Liabilities

Liabilities are a company's debts and other obligations. Things like debts, payments due, and employee salaries that haven't been paid yet are all part of this category. Liabilities can quickly get out of hand if proper measures are not taken.

Current Liabilities

The term "current liability" is used to describe a company's debts and commitments that have a maturity date within one year or the normal operating cycle. These include things like short-term loans, accrued expenses, and accounts payable.

Examples of current liabilities include:

- **Accounts payable:** Amounts owed to suppliers for goods or services received but not yet paid.

- **Short-term loans:** Any borrowings or loans that are due within one year.

- **Accrued expenses:** Expenses that have been incurred but not yet paid, like salaries, taxes, or utilities.

Non-Current Liabilities

Non-current, or long-term, liabilities are debts or obligations that are not expected to be settled within the next year.

Examples of non-current liabilities include:

- **Long-term loans:** Any borrowings or loans with repayment terms extending beyond one year.

- **Bonds payable:** Debt securities that the company has issued and whose maturities exceed a year.

- **Pension obligations:** The company's commitments to provide future retirement benefits to its employees.

Example 3.16:

Company XYZ Manufacturing has the following liabilities.

Current:

A total of $50,000 is owed to suppliers. The company borrowed $20,000 over six months for renovations. XYZ Manufacturing has $10,000 in accrued expenses.

Total current liabilities

= Personal Accounts payable + short term loans + accrued expenses

= $50,000 + $20,000 + $10,000

= $80,000

Non-current liabilities:

The company has a mortgage of $100,000 and bonds payable in the amount of $200,000. It also has an estimated pension liability of $300,000.

Total non-current liabilities

= long term loans + bonds payable + pension obligations

= $100,000 + $200,000 + $300,000

= $600,000

Total liabilities

= current liabilities + non-current liabilities

= $80,000 + $600,000

= $680,000

Reserves

Reserves are funds that a business sets aside or keeps for particular uses. Reserves are a portion of a company's profits that are not distributed as dividends to shareholders but are instead kept within the company for a number of reasons.

Reserves serve as a financial cushion or contingency for the company and typically:

- Companies may set aside reserves to prepare for unexpected events like an economic downturn, legal disputes, or large-scale repairs or replacements.

- Reserves can be allocated for future capital investments, research and development projects, or acquisitions to support the company's growth and development.

- Certain industries or jurisdictions may require companies to maintain reserves to ensure compliance with specific regulations or to fulfill financial obligations.

Examples of reserves include:

- **General reserves:** These are reserves set aside for general purposes, providing flexibility to the company for various needs that may arise in the future.

- **Contingency reserves:** These reserves are specifically designated to handle unexpected events or contingencies that may impact the company's financial stability.

- **Dividend reserves:** Some companies set aside reserves to accumulate funds for future dividend payments to shareholders.

- **Legal reserves:** In some countries, companies may be required by law to allocate a portion of their profits to reserve accounts to meet legal obligations or protect against potential liabilities.

It is important to know that reserves are different from retained earnings, which represent the cumulative profits of a company that have not been distributed to shareholders. While reserves are specifically earmarked for specific purposes, retained earnings are the overall profits retained within a company.

Example 3.17:

XYZ Services operates in the technology industry and has accumulated profits over the years. To ensure financial stability and support future growth, XYZ Services decides to allocate reserves for two specific purposes: expansion and contingencies.

XYZ Services allocates $500,000 from its profits to the expansion reserve. This reserve acts as a dedicated fund to fuel the company's expansion initiatives and product diversification.

Furthermore, to prepare for unexpected events or financial uncertainties, XYZ Services sets aside $200,000. This reserve acts as a safety net to address unexpected challenges or financial risks that may arise in the future, helping the company navigate through difficult times without disrupting its operations or financial stability.

Equity

Equity refers to the ownership interest or stake that individuals or entities have in a company. It represents the residual interest in the company's assets after deducting its liabilities. In other words, equity is the portion of the company's value that belongs to its owners, or shareholders.

Example 3.18:

ABC Clothing has total assets of $1 million, which include its inventory, equipment, and cash in the bank. The company also has liabilities, like loans and accounts payable, totaling $300,000.

To determine the equity, we subtract the liabilities from the total assets of the company.

Equity

= total value - liabilities

= $1,000,000 - $300,000

= $700,000

In this example, ABC Clothing has an equity value of $700,000. This means that after accounting for all the company's liabilities, the remaining value belongs to the company's owners, or shareholders. The equity represents their ownership interest in the company.

Equity can also be broken up into individual shares or units of ownership, which are usually shown by shares of stock or equity holdings. Shareholders own these shares, and the amount of ownership they have is based on how many shares they own compared to how many shares the company has given out in total. For example, if ABC Clothing has given out 1,000 shares of stock and a customer owns 100 shares, that person owns 10% of the company.

Equity is what the owners' claims and rights are. It shows how much value would still be left for shareholders if all bills were settled.

Cash Flow and Types of Cash Flow

A company's cash flow refers to the movement of money into and out of a company over a specific period. It tracks the inflows and outflows of cash, showing how much money is coming in from various sources and how much is going out to cover expenses.

There are three types of cash flow that help analyze a company's financial health:

Operating Cash Flow

It shows how much cash a business makes from its daily operations. Operating cash flow is important because it shows how well the main operations of a business are making money. When a company has a positive operating cash flow, it means that it makes more money from its daily operations than it spends. This is usually a good sign.

Example 3.19:

ABC Bakery sells freshly baked goods to customers. In a given month, ABC Bakery receives $10,000 in cash from selling its products. During the same month, the company spends $8,000 on operating costs like ingredient costs, employee wages, and rent.

To calculate the operating cash flow, subtract operating expenses from the cash received from sales:

Operating cash flow

= cash inflow from operating activities - cash outflow from operating activities

= $10,000 - $8,000

= $2,000

In this example, ABC Bakery has a positive operating cash flow of $2,000. This means that after deducting operating expenses from the cash received from sales, the company has $2,000 left as cash flow.

Investing Cash Flow

Investing cash flow refers to cash used or generated from investment activities. It reflects the cash flows from the sale of long-term assets, investments in other companies, or any other capital-intensive activity. A positive investing cash flow is a good indicator that a company is investing in assets or ventures that have the potential to generate future benefits.

Example 3.20:

XYZ Manufacturing decides to purchase new equipment for $50,000 during a specific period. In this case, $50,000 would be considered cash spent in the investing cash flow category. The cash is used to invest in a long-term asset that is expected to provide benefits over several years.

On the other hand, if XYZ Manufacturing sells an old piece of machinery for $20,000 during the same period, the $20,000 received from the sale would be considered an inflow of cash in the investing cash flow category as the cash is generated from selling a long-term asset.

Monitoring their investment cash flow is a way companies can evaluate their capital allocation decisions and assess the potential return on their investments.

Financing Cash Flow

Financing cash flow refers to the cash received and spent associated with financing activities. It reflects the cash flows relating to raising or repaying capital, issuing or repurchasing stocks, and paying dividends to shareholders.

Example 3.21:

ABC Corporation borrows $100,000 from the bank for its expansion plans. This cash received represents funds to support the company's operations or growth. During the same period, ABC Corporation decides to repay a portion of its mortgage in the amount of $50,000. This amount is considered an outflow of cash in the financing cash flow category.

Another example is the payment of dividends to shareholders. If ABC Corporation distributes $20,000 as dividends to its shareholders, this cash is also spent in the financing cash flow category.

The financing cash flow is calculated by taking into account all cash received and spent in relation to financing activities.

The overall cash flow of a company is determined by taking into account the cash flows from operating, investing, and financing activities. A positive cash flow indicates that the company is generating more cash than it is spending, while a negative cash flow suggests that the company is spending more cash than it is generating.

Quiz

1. **What word would you use to describe the financial assets that a company owns or controls?**

    (A) Liabilities

    (B) Equity

    (C) Assets

    (D) Revenues

2. **Which of the following represents the financial obligations or debts of a company?**

    (A) Revenues

    (B) Expenses

    (C) Assets

    (D) Liabilities

3. **What is the term for the difference between the total assets and total liabilities of a company?**

    (A) Equity

    (B) Revenues

    (C) Expenses

    (D) Liabilities

4. Which of the following best describes the revenue a company generates from its regular business operations?

(A) Assets

(B) Liabilities

(C) Equity

(D) Revenues

5. What phrase best describes the expenses a business incurs in order to generate revenue?

(A) Liabilities

(B) Assets

(C) Expenses

(D) Revenues

6. Assume you have the following financial information for Company ABC:

- Cash: $50,000
- Accounts receivable: $30,000
- Inventory: $20,000
- Prepaid expenses: $5,000
- Accounts payable: $25,000
- Accrued expenses: $10,000
- Short-term debt: $15,000
- Operating income: $100,000
- Depreciation expense: $10,000
- Interest expense: $5,000
- Income tax expense: $20,000

Based on the given information, please calculate the following:

- Calculate the total value of current assets for Company ABC.
- Calculate the total value of current liabilities for Company ABC.

For the answers to this and the other quizzes, visit

http://MoneyMasterhq.com/Books.

Chapter Takeaway

In this section, we looked at some of the most important words and phrases used in accounting. This chapter gives a detailed explanation of accounting terms. This helps readers understand financial statements, financial evaluation, and other basic accounting ideas.

This chapter talks about a lot of different accounting ideas, such as assets, liabilities, equity, revenues, expenses, and more. If you learn these phrases, you'll have the language and jargon you need to talk clearly in the field of accounting.

With a solid understanding of basic accounting concepts, we can read and analyze financial accounts with confidence. It gives us the tools we need to look at a company's finances, figure out what the best move is, and share that information with those who need to know.

Segue to the Next Chapter

In the next chapter, we'll talk about the most basic financial statements used in an accounting system. There is a detailed discussion of financial statements like the balance sheet, income statement, and statement of cash flows, as well as their purpose, their parts, and how they work together. This chapter will help us learn more about how accounting information is laid out and used to judge a company's financial situation and performance.

Chapter 4:

Basic Accounting Statements

In this chapter, we'll embark on an adventure that will help you understand the fundamentals of financial data. Financial statements are not as boring as they appear at first glance.

Simple financial statements are like taking a business' pulse. The financial statements of a company are like a window into its operations and performance. Accountants use these numbers to tell a story, demonstrating the company's successes and failures along the way.

Let's begin by getting to know the four main characters in the story: the income statement, the balance sheet, the cash flow statement, and the statement of changes in equity. The financial reporting process is heavily reliant on these statements, each of which serves a specific purpose.

On the income statement, the company's income, expenses, and net gain or loss are all shown. It shows how likely the company is to make a profit over a certain time period.

Next, we'll talk about the balance sheet, which is a snapshot of a company's financial health at a particular point in time. It outlines the company's assets, liabilities, and equity to show how healthy and stable its finances are.

Lastly, look at the cash flow statement to see how cash comes in and goes out. It shows the ins and outs of the company's cash flow and shows whether the company can make money and pay its bills. We also discuss on the Statement of Changes to Equity in this Chapter.

In this chapter, we'll look at the stories behind these financial reports by breaking them down into easy-to-understand stories with the help of concrete examples and eye-catching pictures. Put on your seatbelts, channel your inner novelist, and get ready for an exciting ride through the world of basic accounting statements!

Financial Statements: What Are They?

The financial statements of a business show how it makes money and how well it does financially. Audited financial statements that have been checked for accuracy help investors, accounting firms, and government agencies. For-profit businesses' four most important financial statements are the income statement, balance sheet, cash flow statement, and statement of changes in equity. Financial statements for non-profit organizations appear similar but differ slightly. These statements have numerous advantages. Some of the reasons why financial statements are useful are as follows:

- **Assessing Financial Performance:** Financial statements provide a comprehensive view of a company's performance, including revenue, expenses, profitability, and cash flows.

- **Making informed decisions:** Stakeholders use financial statements to make informed decisions regarding investments, lending, and other financial matters.

- **Understanding financial health:** Financial statements help evaluate a company's financial stability, liquidity, and ability to meet its obligations.

- **Facilitate financial planning:** Financial statements serve as a basis for financial planning, budgeting, and setting financial goals.

- **Supporting regulatory compliance:** Financial statements assist in meeting regulatory requirements and complying with financial reporting standards.

- **Analyzing trends and patterns:** Financial statements enable stakeholders to identify trends, patterns, and anomalies in financial data, aiding in strategic decision making.

- **Communicating with stakeholders:** Financial statements are a transparent and standard way to communicate a company's financial position and performance to stakeholders, building trust and confidence.

The Income Statement or Profit and Loss Statement

The income statement, in contrast to the balance sheet, covers a longer period of time, typically a year or three months. The income statement summarizes the company's financial performance in terms of revenue, net income, expenses, and earnings per share.

Revenue

Sales of a company's goods and services result in operating revenue. As one might expect, an automaker's primary source of operational revenue would be the manufacture and sale of automobiles. The lifeblood of any firm is its ability to bring in operating revenue.

The term "non-operating revenue" is used to describe the money made from things that aren't essential to running a company. These earnings are unrelated to the company's main activity. Non-operating income may come from sources such as:

- Earnings on savings deposits

- Earnings from property rentals

- Strategic partnership revenue includes things like royalty payments

- Advertisement revenue earned by a firm via a billboard on company property

The term "other income" refers to cash received from sources other than the main business. Other income could come from selling long-term assets like land, cars, or a company and making a profit.

Expenses

When a business' main action brings in money, it has to pay for its primary expenses. Research and Development (R&D), as well as Selling, General, and Administrative (SG&A) costs, depreciation and amortization, and COGS, are all examples of expenses.

Wages, sales commissions, power, gas, and water are all common overhead expenses.

Interest on loans or debt is one example of a cost that can be attributed to a secondary activity. Losses incurred as a result of the sale of an asset may also be included in expenses.

An income statement's main purpose is to show the financial results of a company's operations, but it can also be used to show if sales or revenue are increasing over time.

Investors can also look at how well management is able to keep costs down. This lets them know if the company's efforts to lower sales costs will lead to higher profits in the long run.

Sample of Income Statement

As of December 31, 2022, the following is an excerpt from the income statement for XYZ Organization's fiscal year 2021.

- Overall, revenues amounted to $163,300.

- The total expense was $120,300.

- The company made $43,000 in net income.

See an example of an income statement below:

XYZ Organization

Income Statement

As of December 31, 2021

Revenues:	$	$
Painting Fees Earned		163,300
Expenses:	$	$
Salaries Expense	66,800	
Painting & Supplies Expense	27,500	
Rent Expense	9,600	
Advertising Expense	3,200	
Depreciation: Painting Equipment	1,200	
Insurance Expense	12,000	
Total Expenses		(120,300)
Net Income		**43,000**

The Balance Sheet

A balance sheet is a financial statement that provides a snapshot of a company's financial position at a specific point in time, typically at the end of a reporting period. It presents a summary of what a company owns (assets), what it owes (liabilities), and the remaining value for the owners (shareholders' equity).

For example, if you take a photograph, it explains something based on that particular moment at which the photograph was taken. The balance sheet is similar; it explains the company's assets, liabilities, and equity at that exact moment.

The date at the top of the balance sheet indicates when the balance sheet was prepared; in most cases, this will be at the end of the reporting period. The sections of a balance sheet are explained below:

Assets

- Liquid assets consist of things like cash on hand or items easily convertible into cash, such as government-issued treasury bills or certificates of deposit.

- A company's accounts receivable are the amounts of money its customers owe it for the purchase of its goods and services.

- Inventory is the stock of items that a firm keeps on hand and is ready to be sold. Products that have been completed, but not yet sent, and unprocessed raw materials are all examples of inventory.

- Prepaid expenses that have been paid before the services are used. Since the corporation has not yet reaped the benefits of these expenditures, they are classified as an asset until such time as they are.

- Businesses hold capital assets, such as real estate, machinery, and equipment, for their ongoing success. Manufacturing facilities and large machinery utilized in the processing of raw materials fall under this category.

- Investments are things you own with the hope of earning a profit in the future. These aren't put to use in production; rather, their value is being saved for future growth.

- Intangible assets, such as a company's trademarks, patents, and goodwill, cannot be seen or touched but will generate revenue in the future.

Liabilities

- Accounts Payable are the bills that must be paid as part of a company's regular operations. This consists of bills for essential services, rent, and commitments to purchase items.

- Salaries payable are cash owed to workers in exchange for their services.

- The terms of a loan, such as the interest rate and repayment period, are memorialized in a note payable.

- Dividends payable refers to dividends that were announced but not yet given to shareholders.

- Any loan with a maturity date more than a year away is considered long-term debt, as are mortgages and other home-equity lines of credit. Keep in mind that this debt is classified as an ongoing liability due to its relatively short maturity.

The Equity of Shareholders

The equity of a company's shareholders is determined by subtracting the value of its assets from its liabilities. After paying off all of the company's debts and selling off all of its assets, the stockholders' equity is the amount of money left over for the shareholders. Retained earnings, which are not distributed to shareholders as dividends, are included in shareholders' equity.

Sample of Balance Sheet

See below for an overview of Rigz Enterprises' year-end balance sheet as of December 31, 2022:

- A total of $380,000 was available.

- The total amount of debt was $150,000.

- A total of $200,000 was invested.

- During the time frame in question, total assets were the same as total liabilities and equity, or $380,000.

The name "balance sheet" refers to the way it always balances based on the equity of Total Assets = Liabilities + Equity, which is illustrated by the below balance sheet.

See the next page for what a balance sheet looks like:

Rigz Enterprises

Balance Sheet

As of December 31, 2022

Assets	Liabilities and Equity
Current Assets:	*Current Liabilities:*
Cash and Cash Equivalents: $50,000	Accounts Payable: $20,000
Accounts Receivable: $30,000	Short-Term Loans: $10,000
Inventory: $20,000	Accrued Expenses: $5,000
Total Current Assets: $100,000	**Total Current Liabilities: $35,000**
Non-Current Assets:	*Non-Current Liabilities:*
Property, Plant, and Equipment: $200,000	Long-Term Loans: $100,000
Intangible Assets: 50,000	Deferred Tax Liability: $15,000
Investments: 30,000	
Total Non-Current Assets: $280,000	**Total Non-Current Liabilities: $115,000**
Total Assets: $380,000	**Total Liabilities: $150,000**
	Equity:
	Share Capital: $100,000
	Retained Earnings: $130,000
	Total Equity: $230,000
	Total Liabilities and Equity: $380,000

The Cash Flow Statement

The Cash Flow Statement (CFS) looks at a company's ability to make cash to meet its financial needs, such as making interest payments, paying its employees, and buying new equipment. The cash flow statement is prepared for a period of time similar to the income statement. The income statement and balance sheet are not complete without the cash flow statement.

Potential investors can use the CFS to learn about a company's activities, cash flow, and expenses. The CFS can also tell you how healthy a company's finances and operations are.

Cash flow statements cannot be calculated with a specific formula. Instead, it's broken down into three sections that detail cash flow for specific needs:

Operating Activities

On the cash flow statement, any cash received or spent as a result of regular business operations, including the sale of goods and services, is categorized as "operating activities." The term "cash from operations" refers to the total of all cash transactions, such as accounts receivable, inventory, depreciation, and account payables. Paychecks, tax returns, interest, rent, and product sales are all examples of cash transactions.

Financing Activities

Money received from investors or banks and used for shareholder dividends is referred to as "cash from financing activities." Debt and equity offerings, stock buybacks, loans, dividends, and principal and interest payments are all examples of financing operations. The cash flow statement connects the income statement and balance sheet by aligning the three primary business operations.

Please refer to the previous chapter for detailed explanations of the terms.

XYZ Organization

Cash Flow Statement

FY Ended December 31, 2021

Cash Flow from Operating Activities		
Net Earnings		$2,000,000
Addition to Cash		
Depreciation		10,000
Decrease in Accounts Receivable		15,000
Increase in Accounts Payable		15,000
Increase in Taxes Payable		2,000
Subtractions From Cash		
Increase in Inventory		(30,000)
<u>Net Cash from Operations</u>		<u>$2,012,000</u>
Cash Flow from Investing		
Equipment		(500,000)
Cash Flow from Financing		
Notes Payable		10,000
Cash Flow for FY Ended 31 Dec 2022		**$1,522,000**

Statement of Changes in Equity

The equity accounts of a company are a representation of the value of ownership in the business, and the statement of changes in equity details the movements of these accounts. This statement, like an income statement, summarizes financial activity for a specified time frame and contains the following sections:

- Earnings and losses for the period, or total comprehensive income

- Fixes to the company's mistakes

- The effect of new accounting standards

- Shareholder dividends paid out during the time frame

- Additional investments made by owners during the period

Changes in retained earnings during the reporting period are reflected here, hence the statement's alternative name: the statement of retained earnings. Retained earnings (or losses), dividends paid to investors, and owner withdrawals are the main components of this report.

Statement of Changes in Retained Earnings

Business ownership can take many forms, from sole proprietorships to partnerships to corporations. Depending on the ownership structure, this statement may have different names. The financial document that sole proprietorships use is the owner's equity statement. A public company that issues stock to investors will have a statement of stockholders' equity or a statement of changes in retained earnings. The reports' names may change, but they all serve the same purpose of reflecting shifts in the value of a company over time.

Depending on the ownership structure, the statement of equity changes may contain different information. Investments and withdrawals by the sole proprietor would fall under this category, while for a corporation it would be share issuances and repurchases. The information presented in this statement captures alterations in the business's value over time.

Depending on the movement in the paid-in capital section, larger corporations may choose to present their financial data using either a statement of stockholders' equity or a statement of retained earnings. A stockholders' equity statement is used when there has been substantial movement in this segment, indicating changes in the amounts contributed by owners. On the other hand, a statement of retained earnings may be used if there is little activity and the only change is in earnings. Since the statement of retained earnings relies on data from the income statement, it must be compiled after the income statement has been finalized.

Statement of Changes in Stockholders Equity

A statement of changes in stockholder's equity is a common financial report in the world of public corporations with many shareholders. This statement shows how the company's value has changed over a certain time frame. A general statement of changes in equity includes both stockholders' equity and owner's equity, regardless of whether the entity is a corporation, sole proprietorship, or partnership. Only businesses that have issued stock to investors are eligible to use the term "stockholders' equity."

An example of a Statement of Changes in Equity:

Example Organization

Statement of Changes in Equity

As of December 31, 2022

Shareholders Equity at January 1 2022:	$	$
Opening balance of Equity	$500,000	
Changes in Equity:	$	$
Net income	$100,000	
Additional investments	$50,000	
Dividends paid		$30,000
Other Comprehensive Income	$10,000	
Closing Balance of Equity	**$630,000**	

Quiz

1. Which financial report details the flow of funds in and out of a business over a given time frame?

(A) Balance Sheet

(B) Income Statement

(C) Cash Flow Statement

(D) Statement of Changes in Equity

2. Which statement depicts the financial health of a business at a given time?

(A) Balance Sheet

(B) Income Statement

(C) Cash Flow Statement

(D) Statement of Stockholders' Equity

3. The income statement details the company's

(A) Assets, liabilities, and equity

(B) Revenues, expenses, and net income

(C) Cash inflows and outflows

(D) Changes in retained earnings over a specific period

4. Which accounting formula describes the format of the balance sheet?

(A) Assets = Liabilities + Revenues

(B) Assets = Liabilities + Equity

(C) Assets = Revenues - Expenses

(D) Assets = Equity - Liabilities

5. Which financial report shows a company's retained earnings?

(A) Balance Sheet

(B) Income Statement

(C) Cash Flow Statement

(D) All of the above

6. **What are the three primary components of a cash flow statement?**

(A) Operating, investing, and financing activities

(B) Assets, liabilities, and equity

(C) Revenues, expenses, and net income

(D) Cash inflows and outflows

For the answers to this and the other quizzes, visit
http://MoneyMasterhq.com/Books.

Chapter Takeaway

In this chapter, we looked at the balance sheet, income statement, cash flow statement, and changes in equity statement. These primary financial statements are essential for determining a company's financial health, profitability, and liquidity.

We began with the balance sheet, which shows the corporation's financial standing as of a specific date. Stakeholders can view the company's equity, liabilities, and assets.

The income statement, also known as the profit and loss statement, was the next topic covered. The income statement summarizes a company's financial performance over a specific time period, including sales, costs, and net profit or loss. It assists us in determining the company's revenue-generating potential and profitability.

We also looked at the cash flow statement, which is a financial document that tracks cash inflows and outflows over a specific time period. The income statement of a company can provide information on cash flow from operations, investments, and financing. One of the most important indicators of a company's capital and financial health is cash flow.

We concluded by looking at the statement of changes in equity, which summarizes the movement of equity accounts over a given time frame. The report illustrates the impact of events and transactions on the company's equity during the specified time period. By tracking changes in equity, interested parties like shareholders, investors, and analysts can gauge the company's financial health and performance.

Learning to read and understand these basic financial statements allows us to become better financial analysts. These statements serve as the foundation for financial analysis, decision-making, and performance evaluation.

Segue to the Next Chapter

The next chapter will delve even deeper into the world of financial analysis, building on the groundwork laid in this one. We investigate accounting ratios, which enable us to draw conclusions by comparing and evaluating a wide range of financial indicators. Furthermore, we'll investigate the incorporation of business analytics, which uses data to assist businesses in gaining insights and making better decisions. We will have a better understanding of how to analyze financial statements and draw conclusions about a company's success and financial condition by the end of this chapter.

Chapter 5:

Data Slicing and Dicing:

Accounting Ratios

Welcome to an enthralling journey into the world of numbers and insights, where financial analysis and practical decision-making collide. This chapter can assist non-finance managers in understanding financial analyses.

Financial analysis is simply the process of making sense of a company's financial data. Don't worry if you're not a math whiz or number nerd; we will explain everything in simple terms. The methods we will cover will range from the most basic to the most cutting-edge in analytics. First, we will go over some fundamental financial analysis techniques, such as horizontal and vertical analysis, variance and sensitivity analysis, standard financial reporting formats, and ratio analysis.

Ratio analysis, in particular, is the foundation of financial analysis. It provides a methodical framework for evaluating a company's financial health and performance by examining the inter-relationships between key financial metrics. We will delve into the world of financial ratios, looking at a variety of metrics that reveal a company's liquidity, efficiency, profitability, and solvency. To aid understanding, we will visually summarize the various ratio types. You will be able to navigate the vast world of accounting ratios and make informed decisions if you use this overview as a guide.

We will analyze and evaluate your data together to uncover hidden insights and unlock the full potential of financial analysis. Join me as we unravel the mysteries of accounting ratios and business analytics, so you can make sound financial decisions for your company. Let's delve in and see what treasures your financial records have!

Financial Analysis: What Does It Mean?

A financial analysis can help an individual, business, or investment opportunity understand their financial situation better. When conducting a financial analysis, we will analyze financial statements like the income statement, balance sheet, and cash flow statement, as well as financial reports and any other relevant information (including non-financial information) that will allow us to make informed decisions and recommendations.

Financial analysis can be used for a variety of purposes, including:

- **Assessment of company performance:** Companies analyze their financial statements to evaluate their financial health, liquidity, solvency, and profitability. This evaluation enables them to identify areas of strength and weakness, make strategic decisions, and improve their financial position.

  Company X, for instance, earns a net profit of $1,000,000, while Company Y earns a net profit of $2,000,000. Company Y may have performed better financially than Company X based on appearances alone, ignoring all other factors. However, drawing this conclusion based solely on net profit may not be prudent. Additionally, each company's revenue, gross margin, and invested capital should be considered. This is where financial analysis could be useful.

- **Creditworthiness evaluation:** Lenders and creditors evaluate the financial information of people or companies to assess their financial standing and potential for default. This research assists with loan choices and setting interest rates.

- **Investment decisions:** Investors examine financial data to determine the profitability, potential growth, and risks associated with investing in a specific company or project. This allows them to make more informed investment decisions.

- **Ratio analysis:** Looks at the relationships between various financial figures and uses them to assess the performance, profitability, and financial health of a company. By analyzing ratios over time and comparing them to industry benchmarks or competitors, stakeholders can gain insights into a company's financial strengths, weaknesses, and trends.

- **Budgeting and forecasting:** Financial analysis is essential when developing budgets, financial plans, and projections for the future. It aids in the establishment of reasonable goals, the estimation of revenues and expenses, and the tracking of progress toward financial objectives.

Shareholders can use the financial analysis to develop better strategies, make more informed decisions, and take the necessary actions to realize their business goals. By assisting stakeholders in developing strategies, making data-driven decisions, and taking the necessary actions, it makes it easier to achieve financial goals.

Different Kinds of Financial Analysis

There are various types of financial analysis, each with a specific focus. It is important to note that financial analysis should not be viewed in isolation; it should be combined with other data to form a complete picture of a company's financial position and future prospects.

The different types of financial analysis are:

- horizontal analysis

- vertical analysis

- financial liquidity

- profitability

- variance

- valuation

Horizontal Analysis

This is also known as "trend analysis," and it examines financial data over time to identify any trends. When we examine financial data in this manner, we can identify patterns and changes. This type of analysis can be used to look at cash flow statements, income statements, and balance sheets, and it can even be used to compare corresponding line items or categories from different periods. Periods can be selected to span months, quarters, or years, depending on what is required from the analysis.

This type of analysis can be helpful in determining growth trends, seasonal variations, sudden changes that may need to be investigated, and future projections based on the trends and patterns observed. It gives a big-picture view of the company's financial stability over time. Remember, when looking horizontally at data, we also need to take external factors like economic conditions and company-specific events into account to interpret the data accurately.

Vertical Analysis

This type of analysis looks at different financial items within a single period. Items are commonly expressed as a percentage of a total, for example, total assets or a balance sheet. Vertical analysis can be very useful to help recognize changes and compare various items. In vertical analysis, each line item is expressed as a percentage of the total. In this way, we can compare items over time and even across companies. It gives a quick overview of an item's relative importance within the larger financial structure. In this way, we can get a better understanding of the relative weight of different income streams, expenses, liabilities, and assets. This information can also be very valuable in identifying patterns and trends connected to a specific item. This allows for an easy-to-understand visual representation of the makeup and basis of a company's financial statements.

Financial Liquidity

Liquidity is about how easily a company can pay its short-term bills, service its loans, and turn its assets into cash. Having good liquidity means the company has enough cash on hand or assets that can easily be turned into cash to handle expenses. To measure liquidity, we compare the company's current assets (things like cash, accounts receivable, and stock) to its current liabilities (like accounts payable or debts due soon). A big part of financial liquidity is having a positive cash flow; in other words, the company has enough money coming in that can be used to service its obligations.

Profitability

Here we look at how well a company is performing in terms of making money and earning profits. It is all about making sure that the company is making more money than it is spending. Financial analysts look at net profit, which is total revenue minus all costs and expenses. They also look at the profit margin, which is the profit, divided by the revenue and expressed as a percentage. In this way, we can determine how much profit the company is making for every dollar it receives. High profitability means the company is making money, while low profitability may be an indicator of challenges. In this way, we can determine the company's performance and look for trends over time. Improving profitability is a common goal for all companies and involves managing costs, increasing income, and finding ways to be more efficient in operations.

Variance

In this part of financial analysis, we look at how the actual numbers compare to the forecasted or expected numbers. It tells us what the difference is between what was predicted or budgeted and what actually happened in the business. This difference can be positive or negative, depending on whether the actual number is higher or lower than what was expected. In this way, we can determine if performance in certain areas was better or worse than expected. Managing variances is important to make sure a business stays on track and achieves its financial objectives.

Valuation

By looking at a financial evaluation analysis, it is possible to determine what a company is worth in monetary terms. There are different methods of valuation, and it will depend on the purpose of the valuation. Some techniques include:

- **Market-based valuation:** This method compares the prices of similar assets that have recently been bought or sold in the market.

- **Income-based valuation:** Here we look at the expected income or cash flow that the company will generate in the near future. It also considers factors like risk and growth potential.

- **Asset-based valuation:** The focus is on the balance sheet and the company's net worth is determined by subtracting its liabilities from its assets.

Financial analysts use valuation to assess the attractiveness of investments, evaluate mergers and acquisitions, and analyze the performance of companies. It may be important to remember that valuation is not an exact science as it makes assumptions about various factors, like market conditions and economic factors, that can impact the value of an asset.

Moving Beyond Analyses to Analytics

In today's dynamic business environment, the evolution from analysis to analytics is of greater importance than ever. Data examination for the purpose of drawing conclusions is the essence of analysis. The key is to analyze the data, spot trends, and draw reasonable conclusions based on what you find. However, as time goes on and more data is collected, more needs to be analyzed.

Analytics is a new and intriguing area that extends far beyond traditional methods of analysis. Analytics is the process of using sophisticated methods to dig deeper into data and release its latent value. It's like looking at something through a magnifying glass; you get to see finer details and make connections you might have missed before. The focus of analytics is on extracting actionable information or predictive capabilities from the data.

While both produce valuable results, analytics goes further by employing innovative techniques. Methods such as statistical modeling, machine learning, and data visualization are used to find insights into mountains of raw data.

An entire decision-making paradigm has shifted with the advent of analytics as opposed to traditional "analysis." It enables organizations to ditch antiquated methods in favor of a more modern, data-centric perspective. Better predictions, new opportunities, streamlined operations, and a leg up on the competition are just some of the benefits that analytics can bring to businesses.

Key Ideas in Analytics

This section will focus on the fundamental ideas and real-world applications of analytics. We'll dive into how companies can use data to make smarter choices and discover untapped opportunities.

Unlocking the Full Potential of Data

Data is the star of the show in the analytical world. It's a veritable gold mine of opportunity just waiting to be uncovered. Successful firms recognize the importance of data and use it to their advantage to better understand their operations, customers, and target markets. With more data, we can make better choices, develop more effective tactics, and chart a course for the future.

Statistical Models: Understanding Complexity

In the analytic toolkit, statistical models are among the most potent weapons. By revealing hidden patterns and connections, they help in the interpretation of large data sets. With the use of these models, organizations can confidently anticipate future outcomes, identify emerging patterns, and identify the most important contributors to their success or failure. Businesses can better deal with uncertainty and make decisions based on facts if they use statistical models.

Machine Learning's Untapped Potential

Machine learning, a branch of artificial intelligence (AI), helps companies mine massive datasets for actionable intelligence. It entails teaching computers to draw valid conclusions or predictions from data on their own. Organizations can automate tasks, enhance operations, and tailor services to individual customers by employing machine learning methods. Machine learning's strength resides in its capacity for ongoing learning and adaptation, both of which improve its performance and the quality of the results it produces.

Visualizing Data to Understand Its Meaning

Data visualization is the process of turning raw data into a visual representation of its meaning. Making dashboards, charts, and other visual representations of previously unintelligible data is required. For businesses, visualizations make it simpler to share information, identify trends quickly, and comprehend what is happening. When data is presented visually, it helps stakeholders better understand its value and bridges the gap between the data and practical insights.

Year	Profit (US $)
Year 1	100,000
Year 2	125,000
Year 3	185,000
Year 4	210,000
Year 5	225,000

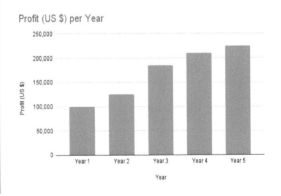

Decision-Making Based on Facts

Data-driven decision-making is the ultimate goal of analytics. Making decisions based on evidence rather than gut instinct is encouraged. Data-driven decision-making helps businesses eliminate prejudice, lessen vulnerability, and maximize returns. It allows for a more detached and comprehensive view of issues, improving the likelihood that choices will contribute to business objectives.

By incorporating the five key tenets of analytics mentioned above, companies can maximize the value of their data. They can help you distill the vast amounts of available data into useful insights that will guide your next round of strategic decisions. Success in today's data-driven world is founded on insights and comprehension, and analytics equips businesses to gain both.

How Does Financial Analysis Work?

The key ideas in analytics lay the foundation for understanding how financial analysis works. By examining concepts such as data interpretation, statistical models, and the visualization of data, we gain valuable insights into the effectiveness of analytics in the financial realm. Armed with these key concepts, we can investigate the process of financial analysis, which entails the application of analytical techniques to evaluate financial data, identify patterns, evaluate performance, and make informed decisions. This section will examine the methodologies, tools, and metrics used in financial analysis, highlighting the ways in which analytics can uncover valuable information and drive strategic decision-making in the dynamic financial world.

Analyzing the deviations between expected and realized results is what variance analysis does. To do this, it is common practice for businesses to forecast sales for the coming year and then evaluate their actual sales revenue against their forecast. Depending on the needs of the company, variance measurements could be performed on a monthly, quarterly, or annual basis.

The more frequently an organization monitors these differences, the greater the possibility that it will notice patterns in its data. Whether or not a variance is successful can hinge on the sort of variance analysis calculated and the anticipated variations in the business. Companies using this method of analysis can determine the following types of variance:

- Sales variance

- Purchase variance

- Material variance

- Overhead variance

- Efficiency variance

- Labor variance

A Deeper Dive Into Variance Analysis and Its Variants

Your choice of variance analysis method should be tailored to the data at hand. There are three primary ways to examine variance:

Labor Variance

Labor variance is the difference between the expected labor cost and the actual labor cost incurred by the company. A positive labor variance could happen if employees worked more efficiently or if the wage rates were lower than expected. A negative labor variance, where labor costs more than expected, can be due to things like overtime wages, unexpected staffing requirements, or wage increases.

By analyzing labor variance, a company can better understand the differences and take the appropriate actions. A business may make adjustments to labor planning and resource allocation if the labor variance is negative. The formulas for calculating both individual and aggregate labor variations are as follows (Tamplin, 2023a):

- Overall variance = Rate variance + Efficiency variance

- Efficiency variance = (Actual hours x Standard rate) − (Standard hours x Standard rate)

- Rate variance = (Actual hours x Actual rate) − (Actual hours x Standard rate)

Material Variance

Material variance refers to the difference between the expected or budgeted cost of materials and the actual cost incurred by the company. The quantity of materials needed and the cost of those materials are two factors that affect this variance. If more material is used than expected or if the price of material is higher than budgeted for, a negative material variance will follow. When a negative variance is discovered, a company must investigate the causes and make the necessary adjustments. This type of analysis is important for managing costs and making sure that budgets are realistic. It can help businesses control their expenses, manage the use of materials efficiently, and make informed decisions about the sourcing of goods and production methods used by the company. Below are some formulas used to calculate material cost variance and material price variance (Tamplin, 2023c):

- Overall variance = Quantity variance + Price variance

- Price variance = (Actual quantity x Standard price) − (Actual quantity x Actual price)

- Quantity variance = (Actual quantity x Standard price) − (Standard quantity x Standard price)

Overhead Variance

Overhead variances can be fixed or variable. A fixed overhead variance is a cost that the company bears; it is unaffected by the volume of production or sales. Examples of fixed overheads include things like rent, salaries for employees not directly involved in production, and insurance. A negative variance in the fixed overheads can happen when the fixed overhead costs are higher than expected due to factors like unexpected increases in rent, utilities, or other unforeseen costs. When this variance is detected, the company needs to determine the reason, adjust its budget accordingly, and look at ways to operate more efficiently. Variable overhead costs include things like direct labor costs, raw material costs, and utilities that vary based on production levels. A negative variance may indicate the need for a company to evaluate its production processes and inventory management. Some calculations to help you calculate overhead variances are (Tamplin, 2023b):

- Budget variance = Actual fixed overhead cost − Budgeted fixed overhead cost

- Budgeted fixed overhead cost = Denominator level of activity x Standard rate

- Volume variance = Budgeted fixed overhead cost − Fixed overhead cost applied to inventory

- Fixed overhead cost applied to inventory = Standard hours x Standard rate

- Overall variance = Budget variance + Volume variance

Using Variance Analysis: Some Examples

Calculations typical of a variance analysis are as follows:

Labor Variance Example:

Crown Builders budgeted for 500 hours of labor at an expected rate of $20 per hour, resulting in a total expected labor cost of $10,000. However, the actual labor hours worked were 550 hours, and the actual rate paid to employees was $22 per hour. To calculate the labor variance:

Labor Rate Variance:

Labor rate variance
= (Actual hours x Actual rate) − (Actual hours x Standard rate)
= (550 x $22) - (550 x $20)
= $12,100 - $11,000
= $1,100

In other words, the company paid $1,100 more than it budgeted for on labor costs.

Labor Efficiency Variance

Efficiency variance
= (Actual hours x Standard rate) − (Standard hours x Standard rate)
= (550 x $20) - (500 x $20)
= $11,000 - $10,000
= $1,000

In other words, the company had to pay for 50 extra hours it had not budgeted for.

Total Labor Variance

Total labor variance
= labor rate variance + labor efficiency variance
= $1,100 + $1,000
= $2,100

This number represents the overall difference between the actual labor costs and the expected or budgeted labor costs. It is clear that the company will need to reassess its budget for labor for future projects.

Material Variance Example

ABC Manufacturing budgeted to produce 1,000 widgets and estimated the material cost per unit at $5, bringing the total expected cost to $5,000. However, the actual production resulted in 1,200 widgets, and the actual material cost per unit was $6.

To calculate the material variance:

Material Price Variance

Material price variance
= (Actual quantity x Standard price) − (Actual quantity x Actual price)
= (1,200 x $6) - (1,200 x $5)
= $7,200 - $6,000
= $1,200

This shows the difference between the actual price paid per unit and the expected or budgeted price per unit.

Material Quantity Variance

Material quantity variance
= (Actual quantity x Standard price) − (Standard quantity x Standard price)
= (1,200 x $5) - (1,000 x $5)
= $6,000 - $5,000
= $1,000

This shows the difference between the expected quantity of material and what was actually used.

Total Material Variance

Total material variance

= material price variance + material quantity variance

= $1,200 + $1,000

= $2,200

This represents the difference between the actual and budgeted material costs based on price and quantity. The purpose of segmenting the variance in this manner is to delve deeper into the underlying causes of the variance, such as whether it was caused by price and/or quantity fluctuations.

Fixed Overhead Example

ABC Manufacturing budgeted for fixed overhead costs of $10,000 for the production of 1,000 widgets. The actual fixed overhead costs during production were $12,000.

To calculate the fixed overhead variance:

Fixed overhead variance

= actual fixed overhead costs - budgeted fixed overhead costs

= $12,000 - $10,000

= $2,000

In this example, the fixed overhead variance for ABC Manufacturing is $2,000. The actual fixed overhead costs were higher than the budgeted costs, so the variance is unfavorable and the company needs to reassess their budget.

Analysis of Sensitivity

An analysis of the sensitivity to changes in one or more independent variables, given some initial conditions and hypotheses, is the essence of a sensitivity study. Sensitivity analyses, to put it another way, investigate the relative contributions of several sources of uncertainty to the total uncertainty of a mathematical model. This method is implemented within carefully constructed constraints that are determined by a number of input parameters.

Sensitivity analysis has applications in economics and business. Analysts in finance and economics commonly use this technique, which is frequently referred to as a "what-if analysis."

Changes to one set of data, called input variables, might have varying degrees of impact on another set of variables, or "target variables," in a financial model. It's a method for foreseeing the results of a choice when only some of the possible outcomes are known. An analyst can learn how a shift in a single variable impacts a result by first constructing a specific collection of variables.

When doing a sensitivity analysis, it is necessary to examine both the dependent and independent variables, also known as the target and input, in detail. The analyst considers not just how the input variable influences the outcome, but also how the variables themselves move.

Predictions of public firms' share values can benefit from sensitivity analysis. Earnings, share count, debt to equity (D/E), and industry competition are just a few of the factors that might influence stock prices. Altering the starting assumptions or including new variables can improve the prediction of stock values in the future. The impact of interest rate shifts on bond prices may also be calculated with this model. In this scenario, interest rates serve as the independent variable, while bond prices represent the dependent variable.

Sensitivity analysis paves the way for accurate predictions to be made from actual past data. The success of enterprises, the economy, and financial investments all hinge on thoroughly considering all relevant factors and their potential results.

Illustration of a Sensitivity Analysis

Imagine you are a small bakery owner considering the introduction of a new line of specialty cupcakes. You estimate the initial investment cost, expected sales revenue, and variable costs such as ingredients and packaging. However, there is uncertainty regarding the demand for these specialty cupcakes and how it will impact your profitability. To conduct a sensitivity analysis, you vary the expected number of cupcakes sold within a specific range, such as 100 cupcakes per week, 200 cupcakes per week, and 300 cupcakes per week. By calculating the net income for each sales volume scenario, you can assess the sensitivity of your project's profitability to changes in cupcake sales. This analysis allows you to identify the sales volume level that yields the highest profitability and helps you make informed decisions about pricing, marketing strategies, and resource allocation for the new cupcake line.

A Financial Statement of Common Size

Items on a standard-sized financial statement are shown as percentages of a single, consistent metric, such as total sales revenue. Comparisons can be made across businesses or time periods within the same business with this financial statement format. It's possible that comparing two businesses that employ different accounting methods would yield misleading results.

Despite the fact that most businesses do not present their financials in a standardized manner, it is helpful for analysts to be able to compare the performance of businesses that vary in size or that operate in different economic sectors. This method of presenting financial statements facilitates the study of a company across time and decreases the possibility of bias. Using this method, you can determine how much of the revenue is attributable to the cost of goods sold and how that share has changed over time. A normal set of financial statements would consist of an income statement, balance sheet, and statement of cash flows (as you learned in the previous chapters).

Common-size financial statements turn all the numbers into one number that is easy to compare, such as a portion of sales or assets. There is a slight difference between the methods used to standardize numbers in the various financial statements.

A Common Size Income Statement From Real Life

For instance, if a business has a straightforward income statement that details gross sales of $150,000, cost of goods sold of $75,000, taxes of $2,500, and net income of $72,500, then the common size statement for that business would look as follows:

Income Statement (Common Size)

Item	Amount	Percentage
Gross sales	$150,000	100.00%
Cost of goods sold	$75,000	50.00%
Taxes	$2,500	1.67%
Net income	$72,500	48.33%

Ratio Analysis

Ratio analysis is a way to find out about a business' liquidity, efficiency, and profitability by looking at its financial statements. The fundamental study of a company's equity begins and ends with ratio analysis.

By examining a company's past and present financial statements, analysts and investors use ratio analysis to determine its financial health. Data comparisons can show the evolution of a company's performance over time and help forecast its future prospects. This information can be used to evaluate a company's performance relative to its competitors in the same field as well as to compare the company's financial health to that of the industry as a whole.

Simple for investors to use, all the numbers needed to compute the ratios can be found in the financial statements of a company.

Corporate ratios serve as yardsticks for evaluation. They do sector-specific stock analysis. In the same way, they evaluate present-day performance based on past metrics. Knowing what factors affect a company's stock price and profitability ratios is crucial, as management can sometimes adjust their approach to improve these metrics. Most of the time, ratios are used in conjunction with other ratios rather than by themselves. You may get a better picture of the company and be on the lookout for warning signs if you are familiar with the ratios.

Types of Ratios

Based on the information they convey, the various financial ratios can be categorized into five different sections.

Liquidity Ratios

Liquidity ratios are used to evaluate a company's current and short-term asset position in relation to its current and short-term liabilities. There are a number of different liquidity ratios that can be calculated.

Current Ratio = Current Assets / Current Liabilities

The current ratio assesses a company's ability to meet its immediate financial obligations. If a company's current ratio falls below 1, it suggests it does not have enough short-term cash on hand to pay its immediate debts. The standard cutoff is a number greater than 1.2; however, this can vary by industry.

Quick Ratio = (Current Assets - Inventory) / Current Liabilities

The quick ratio measures a company's ability to pay short-term obligations. The quick ratio is a measure of a company's liquidity and its capacity to satisfy its short-term obligations. If the quick ratio is high, that's a good sign for the business.

Working Capital = Current Assets - Current Liabilities

The working capital ratio is often used to evaluate a business' financial health. When a company's working capital drops to zero or below, it may be experiencing serious financial difficulties. If this happens, the corporation will certainly have trouble paying its debts. We can tell if the company has sufficient short-term assets to cover its short-term debt by calculating its working capital ratio.

Profitability Ratios

Return on Assets (ROA) = Net Income / Average Total Assets

Profitability Ratios are used to evaluate a company's earnings potential in light of its revenue, operational expenses, assets, and stockholder equity. A company's profitability can be gauged by looking at its return on its total assets, or ROA. The return on assets (ROA) reveals how well the management of a company uses its assets to create profits.

Return on Equity (ROE) = Net Profit / Average Owner Equity

The return on equity (ROE) of a company is a measure of the profit it generates using shareholder capital. Return on equity is a measure of a company's profitability. Return on Equity measures how much money a company makes compared to how much money shareholders have put in.

Return on Invested Capital (ROIC) = Net Income + Interest Expense After Taxes / (Total Liabilities + Owner Equity - Current Liabilities)

We can see how profitable the business is by looking at its return on invested capital (ROIC).

Gross Margin = (Sales - Cost of Sales) / Sales

Gross profit margin, also known as gross margin, is a metric used to evaluate a business' health by showing what percentage of revenue remains after deducting the cost of products sold.

Profit Margin = Net Income / Sales

Sales are evaluated for profitability by calculating the profit margin, sometimes called the net margin.

Operating Margin = Operating Income / Sales

The operating margin ratio is a measure of the business' profitability in day-to-day operations before deducting financing costs and taxes.

Earnings Per Share (EPS) = (Net Income - Preferred Dividends) / Common Shares

The earnings per share ratio provides context for a company's success by revealing the portion of earnings that is distributed to each share of capital. Earnings Per Share (EPS) are calculated by dividing net income minus preferred dividends by the number of common shares.

Activity Ratios

Activity ratios are financial analysis ratios that are used to evaluate a company's efficiency in converting its various balance sheet accounts into revenue and profit. Activity ratios can help us understand how effectively a company uses its assets and other balance sheet components.

Assets Turnover = Total Sales / Average Total Assets

An activity analysis is required to determine whether management is making optimal use of available resources. The asset turnover ratio measures how well a company converts its assets into revenue. The higher a company's asset turnover, the more efficiently its assets are converted into cash.

AR Turnover = Sales / Average Accounts Receivables

The accounts receivable turnover ratio comes next, and it gives us an idea of how aggressive the organization is at collecting past-due payments. The average refers to the average between the two financial periods, or by taking the beginning and ending total asset values for a specific period and dividing the sum by two. A healthy value for this ratio indicates that the company is making good use of its assets.

Inventory Turnover = Cost of Sales / Average Inventory

Calculating the inventory turnover ratio allows one to quantify a company's capacity for selling and replenishing its stock over a specific time period.

The fixed asset turnover ratio is a measure of fixed asset profitability. A higher rate indicates that management is making effective use of capital equipment.

Working Capital Turnover = Sales / Average Working Capital

Working capital turnover is the last ratio we'll examine from the activity analysis, and it provides insight into how effectively sales were generated through the use of working capital within a specified time period. This metric can be used to assess the efficiency with which a company is turning its working capital into profits.

Average Working Capital = Average Current Assets - Average Current Liabilities

Capital Structure Ratios

Capital structure ratios, sometimes referred to as financial leverage ratios, are used to assess the equity and debt components of a company. Capital structure analysis helps us establish the optimal mix of debt and equity financing for your company. We expect the debt-equity ratio to change over time as a result of external and internal risk factors affecting the company, as well as the relative prices of debt and investment.

The ratio of a firm's debt to its total assets is the most frequently referenced metric in discussions of capital structure. This ratio emphasizes the level of risk that the company's debt presents.

Debt Ratio = Total Debt / Total Assets

The debt-to-equity ratio comes next. This ratio evaluates the mix of debt and stock financing for an organization.

Debt Servicing Ratio = EBITDA / Total Debt Service Payments

To determine if a corporation can pay its debts, we have to keep track of its ability to meet upcoming obligations, including debt repayments. If you are unable to pay your bills and repayment obligations, you may have to declare bankruptcy.

The debt servicing ratio is one of the fundamental ratios used to assess a company's ability to meet its debt obligations. Included in these payments are both the principal and interest on the debt. The ratio of pretax interest paid on principal, interest, and overdraft is referred to as the debt servicing ratio.

Imagine you have a mortgage or a loan with regular monthly payments. The debt servicing ratio is like evaluating whether your monthly income is sufficient to cover those loan payments. If your income comfortably exceeds your debt payments, you have a high debt servicing ratio, indicating a strong ability to meet your debt obligations. However, if your income is barely enough or insufficient to cover your debt payments, you have a lower debt servicing ratio, indicating a potential challenge in servicing your debt.

In the business context, the debt servicing ratio is calculated by dividing a company's operating income (or EBITDA) by its total debt service payments (which typically include principal and interest payments) over a specific period.

A higher debt servicing ratio indicates a better ability to generate sufficient cash flow to cover debt payments. It suggests a lower risk of defaulting on debt obligations and demonstrates the company's ability to comfortably service its debts.

Times Interest Expense Ratio (TIE) = EBIT / Interest Expense

Imagine you have a personal loan with monthly interest payments. The TIE is like measuring your ability to comfortably cover those interest payments from your monthly income. If your income is significantly higher than your interest expense, you have a high TIE, indicating a strong ability to meet your interest obligations. However, if your income is close to or lower than your interest expense, you have a lower TIE, indicating a potential challenge in meeting your interest payments.

In the business context, the TIE is calculated by dividing a company's operating income (or earnings before interest and taxes, also known as EBIT) by its interest expense.

Market Ratios

Shares of a firm can be under or overvalued, and investors can use market value ratios to help them decide. Management is more concerned with the company's operational performance and, hence, pays less attention to those ratios.

P/E Ratio = Stock Price / Earnings per Share

The Price-to-Earnings (P/E) ratio is a financial metric used to evaluate a company's stock price relative to its earnings. It can provide insights into how the market perceives the company's growth prospects and risk profile. It is important to remember that the interpretation of the P/E ratio should be done in conjunction with other financial and non-financial factors, as a high or low P/E ratio alone may not provide a complete picture of a company's investment potential.

EPS = (Net Income - Preferred Dividends) / Number of Common Shares

Earnings per share (EPS) is the fraction of a company's earnings that are given out to each existing member of the ordinary share capital. The price-to-earnings ratio is calculated by dividing the current share price by the EPS.

Dividend Yield = Dividends Per Share / Share Price

The dividend yield is a financial ratio that measures the return on investment in the form of dividends paid by a company. It indicates the percentage of the current stock price that is paid out as dividends to shareholders.

This ratio helps investors assess the income generated from owning a particular stock relative to its current market price. It is particularly useful for income-oriented investors who rely on dividends for regular cash flow. However, it is important to note that the dividend yield should be analyzed along with other factors such as the company's financial health, dividend growth, and sustainability. A higher dividend yield does not always indicate a better investment, as it could be a result of a declining stock price or an unsustainable dividend policy.

This ratio emphasizes the level of risk that the company's debt presents. Divided by the share price is the yield, or dividend payout per share per year.

Dividend Payout Ratio = Annual Dividends Paid/ Net Income

The dividend payout ratio is a financial ratio that measures the proportion of a company's earnings that are paid out to shareholders as dividends. It provides insight into how much of the company's profits are distributed to investors versus being retained for other purposes. A higher dividend payout ratio suggests that a larger portion of earnings is being paid out as dividends, while a lower ratio indicates that the company retains more earnings for reinvestment or other uses. Again, it is important to consider the dividend payout ratio in conjunction with other factors, like the company's growth prospects, financial stability, and industry norms, to assess the sustainability and attractiveness of the dividend payments.

An Example for Ratio Analysis

The success or failure of a business in the future can be foreseen through the use of ratio analysis. Most profitable businesses have strong ratios across the board, and investors can be quick to dump their shares at the first indication of trouble. Net profit margin, also referred to as "profit margin" or "bottom line," is a metric that financial analysts and business leaders use to compare the relative success of businesses that operate in the same sector. To determine this ratio, take the company's net income and divide it by its sales.

Example 5.1:

Company A:

Return on Assets (ROA): 10%

Debt-to-Equity Ratio: 0.5

Current Ratio: 1.8

Gross Profit Margin: 25%

Operating Margin: 12%

Inventory Turnover: 6 times

Earnings per share (EPS): $2.50

Price-to-Earnings (P/E) Ratio: 15

Company B:

Return on Assets (ROA): 15%

Debt-to-Equity Ratio: 0.3

Current Ratio: 2.2

Gross Profit Margin: 30%

Operating Margin: 18%

Inventory Turnover: 8 times

Earnings per Share (EPS): $3.00

Price-to-Earnings (P/E) Ratio: 20

Now, let's compare these ratios:

- **Return on Assets (ROA):** Company B has a 15% ROA, whereas Company A has a 10% ROA. This indicates that Company B generates profits from its total assets more efficiently than Company A.

- **Debt-to-Equity Ratio:** Company B has a lower Debt-to-Equity Ratio of 0.3 compared to Company A's ratio of 0.5, indicating a lower level of debt relative to its equity financing. This demonstrates that Company B is less dependent on debt financing.

- **Current Ratio:** Company B's current ratio of 2.2 is greater than Company A's ratio of 1.8, indicating a greater ability to cover short-term liabilities with current assets.

- **Gross Profit Margin:** Company B's gross profit margin of 30% is greater than Company A's gross profit margin of 25%. This indicates that Company B is more profitable because it retains a larger portion of revenue as gross profit after deducting the cost of goods sold.

- **Gross Profit Margin:** Company B has an operating margin of 18% compared to Company A's operating margin of 12%. This indicates that a greater proportion of each dollar of revenue remains as operating income after operating expenses have been deducted.

- **Operating Margin:** Company B's inventory turnover is eight times greater than Company A's inventory turnover of six times. This suggests that Company B is more efficient in managing and selling its inventory, potentially avoiding inventory obsolescence and having lower inventory carrying costs.

- **Earnings per Share (EPS):** Company B's EPS of $3.00 is greater than Company A's EPS of $2.50. This suggests that each share of Company B's stock generates a larger profit, possibly indicating a higher profitability per share.

- **Price-to-Earnings (P/E) Ratio:** Company B has a higher P/E ratio of 20, compared to Company A's ratio of 15. This suggests that investors are willing to pay a higher multiple of earnings for each share of Company B's stock, indicating higher market expectations or perceptions of growth potential.

Quiz

1. What does financial analysis mean?

(A) A way to figure out profits and losses

(B) A way to figure out a company's financial health

(C) A way to keep track of personal costs

(D) A way to predict what will happen on the stock market

2. In terms of finances, which of the following is not an example of a Financial Analysis?

(A) Ratio analysis

(B) Trend analysis

(C) Comparative analysis

(D) Linguistic analysis

3. When comparing actual and expected labor costs for a given production activity, which type of variance analysis is most appropriate?

(A) Material Variance

(B) Labor Variance

(C) Fixed Overhead Variance

(D) Efficiency Variance

4. Which kind of variance analysis looks at how much real fixed overhead differs from budgeted fixed overhead?

(A) Material Variance

(B) Labor Variance

(C) Fixed Overhead Variance

(D) Volume Variance

5. Which kind of sensitivity analysis measures how a shift in inputs would affect outputs financially?

(A) Scenario analysis

(B) Common-size analysis

(C) Vertical analysis

(D) Horizontal analysis

6. What are common-size financial statements used for?

(A) To analyze and contrast the financial reports of various businesses.

(B) Examining the percentages of each line item in the financial statements.

(C) To evaluate how susceptible financial statements are to external factors.

(D) To figure out whether or not a business is profitable.

7. Which type of sensitivity analysis entails weighing the likelihood of various outcomes under various conditions?

(A) Scenario analysis

(B) Common-size analysis

(C) Vertical analysis

(D) Horizontal analysis

8. Which category of ratios best reflects a company's capacity to pay its immediate financial commitments?

(A) Measures of liquidity

(B) Ratios of profit to expenditures

(C) Ratios of Action

(D) Ratios of the capital structure

9. **Which ratio best measures how effectively a corporation uses its resources as a whole?**

(A) Liquidity ratios

(B) Profitability ratios

(C) Activity ratios

(D) Capital structure ratios

10. **How can we evaluate a company's profitability in proportion to its sales or investments using ratio analysis?**

(A) Liquidity ratio

(B) Profitability ratios

(C) Activity ratios

(D) Capital structure ratios

11. **Which ratio quantifies the share of debt to equity in a company's total financing?**

(A) Liquidity ratios

(B) Profitability ratios

(C) Activity ratios

(D) Capital structure ratios

12. **Which category of ratios measures the market value and stock performance of a company?**

(A) Liquidity ratios

(B) Profitability ratios

(C) Activity ratios

(D) Market ratios

13. **Which category of ratios classifies the rate at which a firm's assets are turned into revenue?**

(A) Liquidity ratios

(B) Profitability ratios

(C) Activity ratios

(D) Capital structure ratios

14. **When comparing a company's equity to its earnings, what category of ratios best represents the strength of the company?**

(A) Liquidity ratios

(B) Profitability ratios

(C) Activity ratios

(D) Capital structure ratios

15. **Which category of ratios quantifies how quickly current assets can be used to pay down short-term debts?**

(A) Liquidity ratios

(B) Profitability ratios

(C) Activity ratios

(D) Market ratios

16. **Which form of ratio analyzes how effectively a firm manages its working capital?**

    (A) Liquidity ratios

    (B) Profitability ratios

    (C) Activity ratios

    (D) None of the above

17. **Which ratio measures a company's capacity to transform revenue into operating cash flow?**

    (A) Liquidity ratios

    (B) Profitability ratios

    (C) Activity ratios

    (D) None of the above

For the answers to this and the other quizzes, visit MoneyMasterHQ.com/Books.

Chapter Takeaway

Using accounting ratios and business analytics to derive insights from financial data is emphasized as a means to that end in this chapter's final section. With the help of data analysis, we can spot trends and correlations that would have gone unnoticed before, allowing us to make more informed decisions and boost your business's output. These powerful tools allow us to better understand our company's financial situation, profits, efficiencies, and risks, allowing us to make the strategic decisions essential for long-term success in today's competitive business environment.

Segue to the Next Chapter

Now that we've covered the importance of accounting ratios and business analytics, we'll move on to discussing the foundational concepts of accounting in the following chapter, "Key Accounting Terms and Why They Matter." Anyone making financial decisions or conducting financial analysis should be familiar with these fundamental concepts. We'll dive into accounting's foundational ideas, define essential words, and discover how and why they're crucial to conveying an organization's financial health. Come along with me as we explore the role of accounting fundamentals in crafting financial narratives.

Chapter 6:

Key Accounting Terms and Why

They Matter

Welcome to the part on "Key Accounting Terms and Why They Matter." This chapter lays the groundwork for the future study of accounting by introducing fundamental topics. The field of accounting has a reputation for being difficult and overwhelming, but we will explain some fundamental accounting concepts in a language that anyone can understand without resorting to technical jargon.

In this chapter, we'll look closely at four areas of accounting that any non-finance manager or business professional should know. Before diving into the specifics of how cash flows through a business and how that impacts its operations, let's take a closer look at the cash conversion cycle. Having a deeper understanding of this concept will help you streamline your financial operations.

What follows is a breakdown of cash flow versus net income. Although these terms appear to be synonymous at first glance, they actually refer to different aspects of a business' financial health. By comparing cash flow and profit, you can gain a better understanding of the dynamics at play and how they affect business decisions.

Then, we'll define margin and markup for good measure. These two words are similar in meaning, but in the field of accounting, they have very different connotations. Knowing the distinction between these two terms and how they relate to one another will help you analyze pricing and profit margins more precisely.

Finally, we'll compare and contrast cash-based and accrual-based accounting, discussing the advantages and disadvantages of each method. If you are not familiar with the differences between these two accounting procedures, it will be difficult to correctly read financial statements and make educated financial judgments.

When you've finished this chapter, you'll know exactly what each of these crucial accounting terms means and why it matters in the business world. Let's begin the process of unraveling the mysteries of accounting so that we can confidently take on the world of finance and business.

Cash Conversion Cycle (CCC)

A cash conversion cycle (CCC) is an attempt to measure how long it takes for a firm's cash outlay of raw materials to be converted into cash. The cash cycle, or net operating cycle, is another name for this concept. This metric takes into account the time it takes to sell inventory, collect receivables, and settle payables.

The CCC is just one quantitative metric that can be used to measure the effectiveness of a company's operations and management. Decreasing or stable CCC readings over multiple time periods are encouraging, whereas increasing CCC values require further investigation and analysis. Keep in mind that CCC is only useful in sectors where inventory management plays a significant role in daily operations.

The Formula for Cash Conversion Cycle (CCC)

Due to the fact that CCC requires figuring out how much time is spent on each of the aforementioned three parts of the cash conversion life cycle, its formula looks like this:

$$CCC = DIO + DSO - DPO$$

- **Days of Inventory Outstanding (DIO)** (also called Days Sales of Inventory) measures the average number of days it takes for a company to sell its inventory.

  DIO = (Average Inventory / Cost of Goods Sold) x 365

- **Days Sales Outstanding (DSO)** represents the average number of days it takes for a company to collect payment from its customers after a sale was made. It helps assess the efficiency of a company's credit and collection processes.

  DSO = (Accounts Receivable / Total Credit Sales) x 365

  Accounts Receivable represents the amount of money owed to the company by its customers. Total Credit Sales refers to the total value of sales made on credit during a specific period.

- **Days Payables Outstanding (DPO)** measures the average number of days it takes for a company to pay its suppliers for goods or services received on credit. It assesses the company's ability to manage its accounts payable.

DPO = (Accounts Payable / Total Credit Purchases) x 365

Accounts Payable represents the amount of money the company owes to its suppliers. Total Credit Purchases refers to the total value of purchases made on a credit during a specific period.

DIO and DSO represent money entering a corporation, while DPO represents money leaving it. Because of this, DPO is the sole number to the contrary in the equation. Both DIO and DSO can be viewed in a positive light because they are tied to liquid, short-term assets like inventories and accounts receivable. Due to the obligatory nature of accounts payable, DPO is also recorded in the negative.

Cash Conversion Cycle Calculation

There are typically three phases to a company's cash conversion cycle. CCC requires numerous pieces of information from the financial statements, including:

- Data from the income statement, including sales and COGS

- Quantities on hand at the start and finish of the time frame

- The initial and ending accounts receivable (AR) balances

- Invoices due and paid at the start and conclusion of the time frame

- The duration of the time in days (a year has 365 days, a quarter has 90 days, and so on)

In the first phase, the amount of time it will take to sell the company's current inventory is calculated. The day's inventory outstanding (DIO) method is used to derive this value. A lower DIO score is preferable since it implies that sales are being made quickly, which bodes well for the company's turnover.

The cost of goods sold (COGS) is the amount spent obtaining or producing the commodities sold by a business during a given time period, and it serves as the basis for the calculation of DIO, additionally referred to as DSI (days sales of inventory).

DSI = Average Inventory / COGS × 365 Days

Where:

Average Inventory = (BI + EI) / 2

BI = Beginning inventory

EI = Ending inventory

The second phase focuses on ongoing sales and the time it takes to receive the money from those transactions. Calculating DSO involves dividing daily sales by daily revenue, or the average accounts receivable. The shorter the DSO, the better, as it shows the company is collecting capital quickly and adding to its cash position.

DSO = Average Accounts Receivable / Revenue per Day

where:

Average Accounts Receivable = (BAR + EAR) / 2

EAR = Ending AR

BAR = Beginning AR

In the third phase, we analyze the company's current payables. This shows the amount of time the firm has to pay back its current suppliers for the inventory and commodities they have currently supplied the business with. Day's payable outstanding (DPO) is a measure of how long bills and other payables have been overdue. If you can, go for a higher DPO. The higher this figure is, the longer the corporation is able to hold onto cash, increasing its investment possibilities.

DPO = Average Accounts Payable / COGS Per Day

Where:

Average Accounts Payable = (BAP + EAP) / 2

EAP = Ending AP

BAP = Beginning AP

COGS = Cost of Goods Sold

All of the aforementioned data may be found in the yearly and quarterly financial reports that a publicly traded firm is required to submit to the SEC or respective authority of each country. For simplicity, let's assume that a year has 365 days and a quarter has 90 days.

The Financial Insights Provided by the Cash Conversion Cycle

The more inventory a business can sell for a profit, the more money it can bring in. The question then becomes, "How can we boost sales?" Having a steady stream of income makes it possible to increase output and consequently profits by manufacturing and selling a wider range of products. Accounts payable (AP) arise when a corporation uses credit to buy stock.

The company's AR can grow when products are sold on credit.

The Cash Conversion Cycle (CCC) tracks the history of a company's cash transactions. It begins with cash in hand and tracks it as it is used to buy goods and pay bills, then as it is invested in research and development, and finally as it is earned via sales and refunded through receivables. CCC is a measure of how quickly an organization can get from its initial financial outlay to its final profit, and should be as low as possible.

It all comes down to three things for a business to run smoothly: sales realization, inventory management, and payables. Mismanagement of inventory, sales limits, or an increase in the amount, value, or frequency of payables could all spell disaster for a company. CCC takes into consideration the time spent on various procedures in addition to their monetary value, giving an additional perspective on the company's operational efficiency.

Along with other metrics, the CCC value provides insight into a company's financial health in terms of its management's ability to generate and reinvest capital from its short-term assets and obligations. This number is also useful for gauging the operational liquidity risk of a business.

Things to Keep in Mind

If the CCC number is low, that means the company is meeting or exceeding its customers' and market's expectations.

It's possible that a single number representing CCC for a specific time period doesn't tell us too much. It is a tool that analysts use to monitor a company over time and assess it in comparison to its rivals. Monitoring a company's CCC over several quarters can help determine whether its operational efficiency is improving, staying the same, or declining.

Investors may consider a number of criteria when deciding which company is the best fit for their portfolio. When comparing two companies with identical ROE and ROA values, the one with the lower CCC could be the better investment. This means the company can achieve the same level of profitability in less time.

The upper levels of the organization also use CCC to make changes to how they handle in-house credit purchase payments and debtor cash collections.

Cash Conversion Cycle: A Real-World Illustration

Depending on the specifics of how a company operates, certain industries may benefit more than others from using CCC. Major retailers like Walmart Inc., Costco Wholesale Corp., and Target Corp. (TGT) have a lot riding on the outcome of the vote because they are the ones that really acquire and manage inventory and then sell it to customers. All of these establishments might have a very high CCC score in the affirmative.

Companies without inventory management requirements are exempt from the CCC. Companies that sell computer programs via licensing, for example, don't have to worry about keeping inventory in order to make sales (and profits). Similarly, CCC does not apply to insurance or brokerage firms because they do not engage in wholesale purchases for resale.

Some companies, such as e-commerce giants Amazon Inc. (AMZN) and eBay Inc. (EBAY), have negative CCCs. It is common practice for online marketplaces to collect payment for products sold but delivered by independent merchants. These businesses may have a monthly payment schedule or base payments on a certain sales level instead of paying suppliers immediately.

By using this method, businesses are able to prolong their cash hoarding and thus experience a negative CCC. Most E-Commerce sites never keep any stock on hand if the customer receives the goods straight from a third-party vendor.

According to a blog post by Harvard Business School Misamore (2018), CCC had a significant impact on Amazon's survival during the dot-com boom of 2000. The corporation found that negative CCC operations were actually cash flow positive.

Cash and Profit

Profit

Profit refers to the amount of money a business earns after accounting for all its expenses. It's the net result of revenues (money earned from selling products or services) minus expenses (costs associated with running the business). Profit is an accounting concept that's reported on the income statement and gives an indication of a company's financial performance over a specific period (e.g., a month, quarter, or year).

Example 6.1:

Imagine you own a bakery. In one month, you sell $10,000 worth of baked goods and incur $7,000 in expenses (ingredients, rent, utilities, salaries, and so on.). Your profit for the month would be $3,000 ($10,000 in revenue - $7,000 in expenses).

Cash Flow

Cash flow represents the actual inflow and outflow of cash in a business during a specific period. Unlike profit, cash flow focuses on the timing of cash transactions, such as when customers pay for products or services and when the business pays its bills. Cash flow is reported on the cash flow statement and helps businesses understand their liquidity (i.e., the ability to meet short-term obligations and fund ongoing operations).

Example 6.2:

Continuing with the bakery example, let's say your customers don't always pay upfront for their orders. Some customers pay on credit and settle their invoices 30 days after the purchase. In this case, even though you've earned $10,000 in revenue, you might not have received all the cash yet. If you've only collected $8,000 in cash payments and spent $7,000 on expenses, your cash flow for the month would be $1,000 ($8,000 in cash received - $7,000 in cash spent).

In summary, while profit provides an overview of a company's financial performance, cash flow focuses on the actual movement of cash and its impact on liquidity. Both profit and cash flow are important for a business, but they serve different purposes. Profit helps evaluate the overall financial health and profitability of a company, while cash flow helps assess the company's ability to meet its short-term financial obligations and fund ongoing operations.

Markup vs Margin

Markup and margin are essential concepts for non-financial managers to understand in order to make up-to-date pricing decisions, analyze profitability, control costs, effectively plan for the future, and evaluate results.

Markup

Markup is the amount added to the cost of a product to determine its selling price. It's expressed as a percentage of the product's cost and represents the profit as a portion of the cost. Businesses use markup to cover their expenses and generate a profit on each sale.

Example 6.3:

Imagine you own a clothing store and purchase a shirt from a supplier for $20. You decide to add a 50% markup to the cost of the shirt to cover your expenses and make a profit. In this case, the selling price of the shirt would be $30 ($20 cost plus $10 markup). The $10 markup represents a 50% markup on the cost ($10 / $20 = 0.50, or 50%).

Margin

Margin, also known as gross margin or gross profit margin, is the percentage of revenue that remains after accounting for the cost of goods sold (COGS). It represents the profit as a portion of the selling price and shows how much money a business obtains from each sale after covering the direct costs associated with producing or acquiring the product.

Example 6.4:

Continuing with the clothing store example, let's say you sell the shirt for $30 (as calculated with the 50% markup). To calculate the margin, you'll need to subtract the cost of the shirt ($20) from the selling price ($30) and divide the result by the selling price. In this case, the margin would be 33.3% [($30 - $20) / $30 = 0.333 or 33.3%].

In summary, markup is the percentage added to the cost of a product to determine its selling price, while margin is the percentage of revenue that remains after accounting for the cost of goods sold. Both markup and margin are important for a business, but they serve different purposes. Markup helps businesses set their selling prices to cover expenses and generate a profit, while margin helps evaluate the profitability of each sale and compare the performance of different products or businesses within the same industry.

Comparing Accrual and Cash Basis Accounting

The recognition of revenues and expenditures is the primary distinction between accrual and cash-basis accounting. The difference between the cash method and the accrual approach is that the former recognizes income and costs when cash is actually exchanged, while the latter recognizes revenues when earned and expenses when incurred, regardless of the timing of the related cash flows.

Accrual-Based Accounting

Accrual-based accounting recognizes revenue when it is earned and expenses when they are incurred, regardless of when cash is received or paid. This method provides a more accurate picture of a company's financial health, as it reflects the company's financial activities in the period in which they occur.

Advantages:

- Provides a more accurate representation of a company's financial performance.

- Aligns with the matching principle, which states that revenues and expenses should be reported in the same period they are earned or incurred.

- Required by Generally Accepted Accounting Principles (GAAP) for businesses with annual sales above a certain threshold or publicly traded companies.

Disadvantages:

- More complex than cash basis accounting, as it requires tracking receivables and payables.

- May not accurately reflect cash flow, as it records transactions regardless of when cash is exchanged.

Cash-Based Accounting

Cash-based accounting recognizes revenue when cash is received and expenses when cash is paid. This method is simpler than accrual-based accounting and provides a clearer picture of a company's cash flow. However, it may not accurately reflect the financial performance of a business over time, as it doesn't account for outstanding receivables or payables.

Advantages:

- Simpler to implement and maintain, as it doesn't require tracking receivables and payables.

- Provides a clear picture of a company's cash flow, as it records transactions only when cash is exchanged.

Disadvantages:

- May not accurately represent a company's financial performance, as it doesn't account for outstanding receivables or payables.

- Not compliant with GAAP, which may limit its use for larger businesses or publicly traded companies.

In summary, accrual-based accounting provides a more accurate representation of a company's financial performance by recognizing revenues and expenses when they are earned or incurred, while cash basis accounting is simpler and focuses on the actual cash inflows and outflows. The choice between these two methods depends on factors such as the size and nature of the business, regulatory requirements, and the company's financial reporting needs.

Example 6.5:

Let's use a simple numerical example to illustrate the difference between accrual and cash-based accounting:

Suppose you own a small consulting firm. In December 2021, you signed a contract for a project worth $5,000 and completed the work by the end of the month. However, the client agreed to pay you in January 2022. Additionally, you received an invoice for office supplies worth $500 in December 2021, but you plan to pay it in January 2022.

Here's how the transactions would be recorded under both accounting methods:

Accrual Basis Accounting:

Revenue: You would record the $5,000 revenue in December 2021, as the work was completed in that month.

Expenses: You would record the $500 expense in December 2021, as you received the invoice in that month.

Profit: Your profit for December 2021 would be $4,500 ($5,000 revenue - $500 expense).

Cash Basis Accounting:

Revenue: You would record the $5,000 revenue in January 2022, as you received the payment in that month.

Expenses: You would record the $500 expense in January 2022, as you paid the invoice in that month.

Profit: Your profit for December 2021 would be $0 (no revenue or expenses recorded in that month).

This example demonstrates the key differences between accrual and cash-based accounting. Under accrual-based accounting, you recognize revenue and expenses when they are earned or incurred, which provides a more accurate representation of your company's financial performance during a specific period. On the other hand, cash-based accounting focuses on the actual cash inflows and outflows, which can result in a less accurate picture of your company's financial performance over time but offers a clearer view of its cash flow.

Quiz

1. **When measuring cash flow, what exactly is the Cash Conversion Cycle (CCC)?**

   (A) The length of time it takes for a business to turn its cash flow into a profit

   (B) Measures the time it takes for a company to convert its investments in inventory and other resources into cash flow from sales

   (C) The length of time it takes for a business to turn its accounts payable into cash

   (D) The length of time it takes for a business to turn its receivables into cash

2. **Which of the following is not part of the Cash Conversion Cycle (CCC) formula?**

   (A) Accounts payable period

   (B) Accounts receivable period

   (C) Inventory turnover period

   (D) All of the above

3. **During the course of a year, a business has 30 days to collect on receivables, 60 days to sell inventory, and 45 days to pay suppliers. How long does it take to convert its cash flow?**

   (A) 15 days

   (B) 30 days

   (C) 45 days

(D) 75 days

4. What are the advantages of a corporation having a shorter cash conversion cycle (CCC)?

(A) It increases available funds and increases liquidity

(B) It makes more money and brings in more money

(C) It makes less money from outside sources necessary

(D) All of the above

5. Which of the following is not true regarding cash and profit?

(A) In any given company, cash on hand is equivalent to profit.

(B) Unlike profit, which is a measure of financial success, cash represents the real inflows and outflows of money.

(C) Cash is a measure of financial performance, while profit represents the real inflows and outflows of money.

(D) When discussing a company's financial health, cash and profit are used interchangeably.

6. Why is it possible for a business to have positive profits but negative cash flow?

(A) A business with a positive profit margin is one that brings in more money than it spends.

(B) Profits show that the company's finances are in good shape.

(C) Delayed client payments and overspending on investments and inventory might lead to a negative cash flow.

(D) A corporation cannot have negative cash flow if it is making a profit.

7. **Which element of a company's finances is more crucial to its continued success on a daily basis?**

(A) Flow of money

(B) Margin of profit

(C) The margin of profit and the cash flow are of equal significance

(D) All of the above

8. **When comparing margin and markup, what is the primary distinction?**

(A) Markup is a monetary amount, while margin is a percentage.

(B) Margin is the gap between the price at which something is sold and the cost, while markup is the percentage that is added to the cost.

(C) The margin determines product prices, whereas the markup determines revenue.

(D) Margin is determined before costs, while markup is determined afterward.

9. **The manufacturing cost of a product is $50, while the retail price is $80. What is the profit margin on this item?**

(A) $30

(B) 30%

(C) $50

(D) 50%

10. If the cost of production is $100 and the markup is 25%, what will the selling price be?

(A) $25

(B) $125

(C) $75

(D) $250

11. Which accounting approach records transactions according to the timing of cash inflows and outflows?

(A) Accrual-based recording

(B) Cash accounting

(C) Both cash and accrual-based reporting

(D) Neither cash or accrual-based accounting

12. Which type of accounting best depicts an organization's financial health and performance?

(A) Cash-based accounting

(B) Accrual-based accounting

(C) Both cash and accrual-based accounting

(D) Neither cash or accrual-based accounting

13. True or false: Under accrual accounting, income and expenditures are recorded at the time they are generated or spent, rather than at the time cash is actually received or paid.

(A) True

(B) False

For the answers to this and the other quizzes, visit http://MoneyMasterhq.com/Books.

Chapter Takeaway

Overall, this chapter effectively elucidates some of the most essential accounting concepts and demonstrates their practical application. Upon completing this reading, you should possess a more comprehensive understanding of how fundamental accounting principles underpin managerial decision-making and financial reporting. Throughout my years of experience interacting with numerous non-finance managers, I have observed that confusion surrounding these terms is quite common. Gaining a solid grasp of the importance of these concepts, as well as employing them accurately and consistently, is pivotal for accurately interpreting financial statements and assessing a company's financial well-being. Armed with this knowledge, you can confidently navigate the realm of accounting and make informed decisions grounded in robust accounting theory.

Segue to the Next Chapter

Now that we have a firm grasp on foundational accounting concepts, we'll be delving into the murky waters of taxation in the next chapter, "The Realm of Taxes." From budgeting to regulations, taxes have a major impact on the functioning of a firm. In the next chapter, we'll delve into the basics of taxation, discussing topics like the many tax classifications, the tax responsibilities of individuals and corporations, and the way taxation affects economic choice. Join me as we break down the complexities of the tax system and learn how taxes affect the finances of groups.

Chapter 7:

The Realm of Taxes

Taxes—the mere mention of the word can send shivers down anyone's spine. But as complex and overwhelming as taxes may seem, they are an inevitable aspect of life and business. In this chapter, we will delve into the world of taxation, breaking down its complexities and discussing how it affects both individuals and corporations. We'll cover tax classifications, responsibilities, regulations, and the impact on economic choices.

When the government assesses a tax on an individual or a business, it is said to be a direct tax. Income, wealth, and property are common targets for these sorts of levies. Understanding the concepts underlying direct taxes can help shed light on how our income and assets factor into the overall tax burden. With this information in hand, we can make smart choices about our future financial strategy and tax preparation.

Direct taxes are taxes levied directly on the income, wealth or assets of individuals or organizations. Income tax and property tax are examples of direct taxes. They are paid directly to the government by the person or organization on whom it is imposed.

On the other hand, Indirect taxes are taxes levied on the production, sale or use of goods and services. The tax burden is not borne by the one who pays the tax to the government, but is passed on to the final consumers when they consume these goods and services. Value-added tax (VAT) and sales tax are examples of indirect taxes.

The tax system also includes deductions made by employees. Typically, an employee's employer deducts taxes from their paycheck. Income tax, SSI payments (in the US), and health insurance premiums are all examples of potential deductions. Understanding the notion of employee deductions helps shed light on the systems that assure tax regulation compliance and the subsequent influence on a person's net income.

The final topic of discussion in this chapter is "compliance," which means following all applicable tax rules and regulations. To prevent fines and other legal trouble, individuals and organizations must have a firm grasp of their respective compliance requirements. To help you manage the complex world of tax compliance, we will delve into the relevance of records, the necessity of filing, and the urgency of tax payments.

Tax brackets and other numbers used in this chapter are for the United States. However, the principles discussed here could be applied in a similar fashion, depending on the regulations in most countries. Make sure to use the tables that the relevant government agency has issued when filing your taxes.

So, buckle up for a ride through the fundamentals of taxes, withholding, and regulations. By the end of this chapter, you will have a firm understanding of the fundamental concepts and terminology pertaining to these topics, putting you on your way to becoming a savvy taxpayer or skilled finance expert. So come on, let's get started!

How Taxes Shape Economic Choices

Consumption habits, labor supply, investment decisions, real estate preferences, and startup activity are all influenced by tax policy.

Taxes on goods and services, such as sales taxes or value-added taxes, affect consumer behavior. Tax increases can reduce disposable income and discourage spending, resulting in lower consumption. Taxation on interest income or dividends, on the other hand, can influence saving and investment decisions by lowering the return on investment. Tax policies also have an impact on corporate and individual investment decisions. Tax breaks, for example, can encourage businesses to invest in equipment, machinery, or research and development. Higher taxes on capital gains or corporate profits, on the other hand, can reduce investment returns and potentially deter business investment.

Income taxes can have an impact on both the incentives for people to work and the supply of labor. Higher tax rates can reduce after-tax income from extra work or overtime, potentially reducing motivation to work longer hours or take on additional work. This has the potential to affect labor force participation and productivity. Similarly, high taxes on business or capital gains can deter entrepreneurship and risk-taking. Tax breaks or deductions for research and development expenses, on the other hand, can spur innovation and investment in new technologies.

As a result, governments must carefully design tax policies to strike a balance between generating revenue and promoting economic growth while taking into account the potential effects on individual and business behavior.

Types of Taxes

Before we go into more detail, let's take a step back and look at the principle of paying taxes. The history of paying taxes dates back to ancient civilizations like Mesopotamia and Egypt, where the purpose was to support the ruling government and finance public works like building infrastructure or funding wars. The modern concept of income taxes began to emerge in the 19th century. In the United States, income taxes were first introduced during the Civil War as a temporary measure to finance the war effort. It was later slightly changed and reintroduced with the ratification of the 16th Amendment to the U.S. Constitution in 1913, establishing a permanent federal income tax.

Today's tax systems are more complicated, with various types of taxes levied at various levels of government (federal, state, and local). Individuals and businesses may be subject to taxes such as income tax, sales tax, property tax, and corporate tax. With the advancement of technology, governments have implemented systems for efficient tax administration and collection. Electronic filing, online payment options, and automated systems, for example, have made tax compliance more accessible to many people.

Direct Tax

Direct taxes are taxes that are imposed directly on people or businesses. The principle is that those who earn more should pay more taxes. The person or organization in charge of fulfilling the tax obligation pays for it. In the United States, income tax is the most common type of direct tax. Income tax is taken out of your paycheck and paid directly to the government. In other words, the individual or organization is directly liable for tax payments. Examples of direct taxes include:

- **Corporate taxes:** These taxes are paid on profits or income. A company that generates revenue deducts expenses (like salaries, rent, and supplies) from its total income to determine its profits. The specific rules and rates of corporate taxes can vary between countries and even within regions or states. Some governments may provide tax credits for investments in research and development or tax breaks for small businesses to support entrepreneurship.

- **Individual tax:** Based on their earnings or profits, both businesses and individuals are required to pay income tax. Individuals fill out tax returns and pay taxes on their earnings, while businesses pay taxes on their profits.

- **Property tax:** The value of real estate that either individuals or businesses own is subject to property tax. Local governments typically assess it and use the proceeds to fund public services such as schools, roads, and emergency response.

- **Death taxes:** These are direct taxes payable by the individual's estate after their death. Estate taxes are imposed on the total value of a person's estate, which includes all their assets at the time of their death. This tax is typically not applicable to estates below a certain threshold. Inheritance tax is imposed on individuals who receive assets from an estate after someone's death. This tax rate varies by state and may also depend on the relationship between the deceased person and the recipient. For example, some states may have lower tax rates or even exemptions for transfers to immediate family members.

Indirect Tax

Indirect taxes are taxes that are imposed on the sale or consumption of goods and services, rather than directly on individuals or businesses. Here are five examples of indirect taxes:

- **Value Added Tax (VAT):** VAT is a commonly used indirect tax imposed on the sale of goods and services. It is charged at each stage of production and distribution, and ultimately paid by the end consumer. Businesses collect the tax on behalf of the government and remit it to the tax authorities.

- **Goods and Services Tax (GST):** Similar to VAT, GST is an indirect tax levied on the supply of goods and services. It is implemented in many countries worldwide and is designed to replace multiple taxes with a unified tax system. GST is collected by businesses and passed on to the government.

- **Excise Duty:** Excise duty is a tax imposed on specific goods produced or manufactured within a country, such as alcohol, tobacco, petroleum products, and certain luxury items. It is usually included in the price of the product and paid by the manufacturer or producer before the goods are sold to consumers.

- **Customs Duty:** Customs duty, also known as import duty or tariffs, is a tax imposed on goods imported into a country. It is levied by the government to protect domestic industries, regulate trade, and generate revenue. Customs duty is typically collected at the point of entry into the country.

- **Sales Tax:** A sales tax is a consumption tax imposed on the sale of goods and services. It is usually calculated as a percentage of the sale price and added to the final cost paid by the consumer. Sales tax rates and regulations vary across jurisdictions.

These examples demonstrate how indirect taxes are applied to the purchase or consumption of goods and services, with the burden of the tax ultimately falling on the end consumer.

Tax Brackets

Individual Tax Brackets

Tax brackets in the United States determine the tax rates that individuals and corporations pay based on their taxable income. Your filing status (single, married filing jointly, married filing separately, or head of household) and your income determine your effective tax rate. Individual income taxation is progressive, which means that the more you earn, the higher your tax rate. Individual tax brackets are divided into several income ranges, each with its own tax rate. As income rises, it is taxed at a higher rate.

Because of changes in tax laws and regulations, the exact income thresholds for each tax bracket are calculated annually. The IRS set the tax rates at 10%, 12%, 22%, 24%, 32%, 35%, and 37% for the current year (2023).

Tax Rate	Single	Married, Filing Jointly	Married, Filing Separately	Head of Household
10%	$0 - $11,000	$0 - $22,000	$0 - $11,000	$0 - $15,700
12%	$11,001 - $44, 725	$22,001 - $89,450	$11,001 - $44,725	$15,701 - $59,850
22%	$44,726 - $95,375	$89,451 - $190,750	$44,726 - $95,375	$59,851 - $95,350
24%	$95,376 - $182,100	$190,751 - 364,200	$95,376 - $182,100	$95,351 - $182,100
32%	$182,101 - $231,250	$364,201 - $462,500	$182,101 - $231,250	$182,101 - $231,250
35%	$231,251 - $578,125	$462,501 - $693,750	$231,251 - $346,875	$231,250 - $578,100
37%	$578,126 or more	$693,751 or more	$346,879 or more	$578,101 or more

Corporate Tax Brackets

Corporations in the United States are subject to a flat tax rate, meaning they pay a single tax rate on their taxable income. The corporate tax rate before 2018 was graduated, with different tax brackets and rates based on income levels. However, starting in 2018, the corporate tax rate became a flat rate of 21% for federal income tax purposes. Some states may have their own corporate tax brackets and rates; as this can vary from state to state, you should make sure of your state's requirements.

Payroll Deductions

Payroll deductions in the United States refer to the amounts taken out of an employee's paycheck to cover different expenses and liabilities. Some payroll deductions are optional and may only be deducted from a paycheck with the employee's written consent, whereas others are mandatory. Employers who fail to correctly withhold these deductions may be held liable for the amounts. These deductions depend on the details an employee provides on their W-4 form, state and local tax forms, benefit selections, and other factors. It is also important to remember that payroll deductions can vary based on where your business is located and where your employees work. Not all states collect income tax, so that can affect the deductions as well.

Additionally, keep in mind that payroll deductions should be accurately documented and clearly communicated to all employees. Employees should be given a pay stub or other form of documentation outlining the deductions and explaining how their net pay is calculated. While employers have a responsibility to calculate and withhold the appropriate amounts for payroll deductions and remit them to the respective entities (like tax authorities or benefit providers) within the required timelines, managing payroll deductions effectively is crucial for maintaining compliance, meeting legal obligations, and ensuring accurate and transparent payroll processes within an organization.

Let's start by looking at payroll deductions from an employer's perspective. As an employer, payroll deductions refer to the amounts that you withhold from your employees' paychecks to cover various expenses and obligations. These deductions are subtracted from employees' gross pay, resulting in their net (take-home) pay. Deductions from the employer's perspective can be either mandatory or voluntary.

Mandatory deductions include federal income tax, state and local income tax, as well as FICA (Social Security and Medicare). Voluntary deductions can be retirement contributions, health insurance premiums, flexible spending accounts (FSAs), or other benefit programs.

Let's take a closer look at the various types of deductions that an employee might see on their pay stub.

Pre-Tax Deductions

These are deductions taken from an employee's gross income before taxes are calculated. These deductions can have the advantage of reducing taxable income, potentially resulting in a lower overall tax liability for the employee. Some examples include:

- **Contributions to retirement plans:** Many employees contribute a portion of their salary to retirement plans such as a 401(k) or 403(b). These contributions are typically made before taxes and can significantly reduce an employee's taxable income for the year.

- **Health insurance premiums:** If an employer provides health insurance, the employee's portion of the premium is frequently deductible before taxes.

- **Flexible spending accounts (FSAs):** Employees can use FSAs to save pre-tax dollars for eligible healthcare or dependent care expenses. Employees who contribute to an

FSA can reduce their taxable income and use the funds for qualified expenses.

Post-Tax Deductions

Post-tax deductions are deductions made from an employee's earnings after taxes have been deducted. These deductions have no effect on the employee's taxable income, but they are deducted from their net (after-tax) income. Examples of post-tax deductions are:

- **Union dues:** If an employee belongs to a labor union, their union dues are usually deducted from their paycheck after taxes have been deducted.

- **Contributions to charities:** If an employee chooses to make charitable contributions through payroll deductions, the deductions are typically post-tax.

- **Wage garnishments:** A court order instructing the employer to withhold a portion of an employee's wages to satisfy a creditor's debt.

Remember, the specific deductions available to employees can vary depending on their employer's policies and the benefit plans offered. The deductions also depend on the employee's individual choices and circumstances.

While employers are responsible for correctly withholding and deducting amounts, employees should review their pay stubs to understand the various deductions and ensure they are correct.

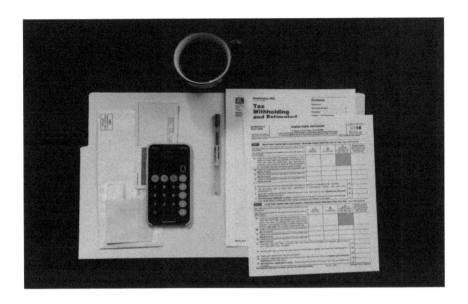

Tax Compliance

In the United States, tax compliance means adhering to and fulfilling tax-related obligations imposed by federal, state, and local tax authorities. Individuals, businesses, and organizations must fulfill their responsibilities to accurately report income, calculate and pay the appropriate taxes, and comply with all filing requirements. Some key aspects of tax compliance in the U.S. include:

- **Identification of taxpayers:** Each taxpayer must have a unique identification number. Individuals usually use their Social Security Number (SSN), whereas businesses use their Employer Identification Number (EIN).

- **Income must be reported from a variety of sources:** This includes wages, self-employment earnings, investment returns, and other taxable transactions. Individuals must file Form 1040 or a variant thereof, whereas businesses must file Forms 1120 (corporations) or 1065 (partnerships).

- **Tax credits and deductions:** Individuals and businesses can claim credits and deductions to reduce their taxable income and overall tax liability. Mortgage interest deductions, student loan interest deductions, charitable contributions, and child care or education credits are examples of these.

- **Filing and payment deadlines:** Taxpayers are required to file their tax returns by the applicable deadlines, which are typically April 15th for individuals. They must also pay any taxes owed by the deadline, which can be done electronically or by mail. If taxes are not filed or paid on time, penalties and interest may be levied.

- **Maintaining accurate records of income, expenses, deductions, and supporting documents is critical:** These records should be kept for a set period of time, usually three to seven years, in case they are required for tax audits or other tax authority inquiries.

- **Taxpayers must follow the applicable tax laws, regulations, and guidelines issued by the Internal Revenue Service (IRS) and state or local tax authorities:** This includes understanding tax obligations, staying up to date on tax law changes, and applying tax rules correctly.

- **Tax audits and penalties:** Tax authorities have the authority to audit tax returns in order to ensure compliance. In the event of errors, discrepancies, or suspected noncompliance, taxpayers may be subject to audits, which include a thorough examination of their tax records and financial records. For intentional tax evasion or significant inaccuracies in reporting, penalties, fines, or legal consequences may be imposed.

It is important for individuals and businesses to consult tax professionals or use reliable and up-to-date tax software to ensure accurate reporting and compliance with tax laws.

Quiz

1. What is the purpose of tax brackets?

(A) To calculate how much tax an individual or business owes

(B) To establish the filing status for taxpayers

(C) To determine eligibility for tax deductions

(D) To calculate the sales tax on goods and services

2. How does the U.S. individual income system work?

(A) It uses a progressive tax structure

(B) It uses a flat rate for all income levels

(C) It imposes a regressive tax on higher income earners

(D) It does not have different tax brackets

3. What is the current corporate tax rate in the United States?

(A) 10%

(B) 21%

(C) 30%

(D) 37%

4. Which statement is true regarding tax brackets?

(A) Higher income is taxed at lower rates

(B) Lower income is taxed at higher rates

(C) Tax brackets only apply to corporations

(D) Tax brackets remain constant and never change

5. **True or false: Tax brackets for individuals and corporations can change over time due to adjustments in tax laws and regulations.**

(A) True

(B) False

Chapter Takeaway

Individuals and businesses must have a thorough understanding of the complexities of taxes, payroll deductions, and compliance in the United States. Taxation is critical for funding public services and infrastructure, and it is critical to navigate the tax system effectively and ethically. Tax compliance entails meeting responsibilities such as accurately reporting income, calculating and paying the correct amount of taxes, and adhering to all filing requirements. It requires staying informed about tax laws and regulations, maintaining proper records, and meeting deadlines. Employers must be meticulous in verifying payroll deductions and remitting withheld amounts to the appropriate agencies.

Payroll deductions, including pre-tax and post-tax deductions, assist in meeting various obligations such as income tax, Social Security, Medicare, and employee benefits. Understanding the various types of deductions and their implications is critical for ensuring compliance and meeting legal obligations.

Tax laws and regulations must be followed in order to avoid penalties, fines, and other legal consequences. Seeking professional advice, using dependable tax software, and staying up-to-date on changes in tax regulations can all assist you in effectively navigating the complexities of tax compliance. Individuals and businesses who understand taxation, payroll deductions, and compliance can fulfill their tax obligations, contribute to society, and maintain financial stability while following the rules and regulations that govern the US tax system.

Segue to the Next Chapter

In the following chapter, we will look at the art of creating comprehensive business plans that include your organization's goals, strategies, and financial projections. We will look at the essential elements of a business plan, such as market analysis, financial forecasting, and implementation. By mastering the art of business planning, you will gain a roadmap to guide your organization's journey, align your team's efforts, attract investors, and make informed decisions about how to navigate the ever-changing business landscape.

Chapter 8:

Business Planning

Whether you are an entrepreneur launching a startup or a seasoned executive leading an established organization, effective business planning, budgeting, and forecasting are vital tools to drive strategic decision-making, financial stability, and sustainable growth. In this chapter, we will look at the core principles and methodologies behind these practices and provide you with knowledge and skills to help you navigate the complexities of the business landscape with confidence.

Business Planning

A business plan is a written document that outlines a company's goals, strategies, and financial projections. It acts as a road map for the organization, providing a comprehensive overview of how the company will operate, grow, and achieve its goals.

Where Are Business Plans Used?

A business plan is a versatile document that should be kept up to date as it serves multiple purposes. Some of its uses include:

- **New businesses:** Entrepreneurs create business plans to document their vision and validate their business concept. This assists in securing funding from investors or lenders. It helps to communicate the business concept, viability of the idea, market opportunity, and strategies for growth and profitability.

- **Business expansion:** Existing businesses that are looking to expand into new markets, launch new products or services, or undertake significant investments use business plans to outline their expansion strategy, financial projections, and potential risks. This helps stakeholders, including investors and lenders, evaluate the feasibility and potential return on investment.

- **Internal planning:** Within an organization, business plans are used for internal planning and decision-making purposes. They provide a roadmap for aligning different departments, setting priorities, and allocating available resources. Business plans help guide management in strategic decision-making, resource allocation, and performance evaluation.

- **Secure financing:** When a company looks at sourcing outside funding, like bank loans, venture capital, or private equity, a business plan is a crucial part of the application process. Lenders and investors analyze the business plan to determine the business' financial health, growth potential, and risk factors. A well prepared business plan increases the chances of securing funding.

- **Partnerships:** Business plans are often shared with potential partners, collaborators, or suppliers to showcase the business' value proposition, growth plans, and the potential benefits of a partnership. It helps to establish credibility and build trust with potential stakeholders.

- **Communication with stakeholders:** Business plans can also be used to share a company's goals, strategies, and financial outlook with stakeholders, including employees, customers, suppliers, and regulatory authorities. It provides transparency and helps align everyone towards a common vision.

The Format of a Business Plan

The format of a business plan can vary depending on the specific requirements of the company. A business plan aimed at investors will have a different focus than one aimed at current stakeholders. However, a comprehensive business plan typically includes the following sections:

Executive Summary

An executive summary is a detailed overview of a business plan, and serves as a snapshot of the key points and highlights the main components of the document. The purpose of an executive summary is to provide busy readers, such as investors, executives, or stakeholders, with a quick understanding of the main ideas and findings without having to read the entire document. An executive summary should be:

- Brief and to the point, typically ranging from one to three pages. The goal is to convey the essential information without unnecessary details or lengthy explanations.

- Even though it is concise, the executive summary should provide a comprehensive overview of the main document. It should cover the key objectives, strategies, market analysis, financial projections, and other crucial aspects.

- The language used should be clear and easily understandable, it should capture the reader's attention and generate interest in the full document.

- The executive summary should highlight the most important findings, conclusions, and recommendations. It should provide a clear understanding of the purpose, significance, and potential impact of the document.

- Furthermore, the executive summary should be able to stand alone as a separate document, providing a meaningful summary even to those who may not read the entire document. It should convey the main message and value proposition of the business plan.

Company Description

A business plan's company description section gives an overview of the company and its key details. It is an opportunity to introduce the company to readers and provide important information about its purpose, structure, history, and distinguishing characteristics. Here are some elements typically included in the company description:

- **Company name and legal structure:** This includes the company's official and registered name, as well as its legal structure, such as sole proprietorship, partnership, limited liability company (LLC), or corporation.

- **Mission statement:** Summarize the company's mission, which outlines its core purposes, values, and the problem or market need that it seeks to address.

- **Vision statement:** Describe the company's long-term vision, including what it hopes to achieve and the impact it hopes to have on the industry or market.

- **Founders and key personnel:** Introduce the company's founders and key management team members, emphasizing their relevant experience, expertise, and roles within the company.

- **Company history:** A brief history of the company, including its founding date, significant milestones, growth trajectory, and notable accomplishments or recognitions.

- **Products or services:** Describe the specific products or services provided by the company. Explain the distinct features and benefits, as well as how they meet customer needs or meet market demands.

- **Target market:** Identify the target market that the company currently serves or intends to serve. This includes describing the characteristics of the ideal customers, their needs, as well as the size and growth potential of the target market.

- **Competitive advantage:** Highlight the company's competitive advantages or unique selling points that distinguish it from competitors. This could include things like proprietary technology, intellectual property, strategic alliances, or specialized knowledge.

- **Business location:** This refers to the physical location of the company, whether it operates from an office, store, or manufacturing facility. If it has multiple locations or an online presence, that should also be mentioned.

- **Legal and regulatory considerations:** Provide an overview of any legal or regulatory factors that may impact the company's operations, such as licenses, permits, industry regulations, or compliance requirements.

Products or Services

A business plan's product or service description section provides detailed information about the specific offerings that the company offers to its customers. It is an opportunity to highlight the features, benefits, and value of the products or services, as well as explain how they meet the needs of customers or solve their problems.

Here are some key components that are commonly included in product or service descriptions:

- **Overview:** Start by providing an overview of the product or service. Give a brief description of what it is and what it does. Describe its main function and purpose.

- **Key characteristics:** Highlight the unique features and characteristics of the product or service. Discuss how it differs from competitors and how it benefits customers.

- **Benefits:** Describe the advantages that customers will receive from using the product or service. Describe how it helps them solve problems, improves their lives, or meets their needs. Focus on the positive outcomes and advantages that customers can expect.

- **Value proposition:** Clearly explain the value proposition of the product or service. This refers to the distinct set of benefits and features that make it appealing to and desirable to customers. Explain why customers should choose your product over competitors in the market.

- **Pricing:** Discuss the pricing strategy for the product or service. Explain how prices are set and how that affects how people see the value of a product. If you have different pricing tiers or options, describe them thoroughly.

- **Intellectual property:** It should be clear if the good or service is subject to intellectual property protection. Patents, trademarks, copyrights, or trade secrets that provide a competitive advantage or protect the company's innovations are examples of this.

- **Development and production:** Describe the process of creating and manufacturing the product or providing the service. Discuss any significant production milestones, partnerships, or resources.

- **Life cycle:** Describe the product's or service's life cycle. Is it a new product, an enhancement to an existing product, or an existing offering? Discuss any future product updates, improvements, or expansions.

- **Competitive analysis:** Provide a competitive analysis of the competitors who offer the same product or service. Determine your direct and indirect competitors and explain how your offering differs from the competition.

- **Future opportunities:** Discuss potential opportunities for product or service growth or expansion in the future. Plans for new markets, features, complementary services, or strategic alliances could be included.

Market Research

This section of the business plan examines the target market, industry, and competitors in depth. It entails researching and analyzing various factors that can affect a company's success, such as market size, trends, customer demographics, and the competitive landscape. Key components typically included in the market analysis include:

- **Industry overview:** This provides an overview of the industry in which the business operates. Describe the current state of the industry, including its size, growth rate, and key trends. Discuss any outside factors that could have an impact on the industry, such as technological advancements, regulatory changes, or economic conditions.

- **Target market:** Define the specific market segments that the company intends to target. Determine the characteristics of the ideal customer, such as demographics, psychographics, and purchasing habits. Explain why this target market is appealing and how the company plans to meet their needs.

- **Market size and growth:** Determine the size of the target market as well as its potential for growth. This can be accomplished by reviewing industry reports, market research, and publicly available data. Calculate the market size using revenue, units sold, or other relevant indicators.

- **Market trends:** Determine and discuss current and emerging market trends. Changes in consumer preferences, technological advancements, regulatory shifts, or industry innovations are examples of this. Examine how these trends can create opportunities or threats for your company.

- **Customer analysis:** Conduct a thorough examination of your target customers. Recognize their wants, preferences, and pain points. Determine how the company can reach and communicate with them effectively. Consider conducting surveys, interviews, or focus groups to gain direct feedback from prospective customers.

- **Competitive analysis:** Evaluate the target market's competitors. Compare the offerings, pricing, distribution channels, and marketing strategies of the company to those of competitors.

- **Unique Selling proposition (USP):** Determine the business' unique selling proposition or competitive advantage. Highlight what differentiates the company from competitors and why customers would prefer its products or services over market alternatives.

- **Market entry strategy:** Describe how the company intends to enter the market. Pricing strategies, distribution channels, marketing campaigns, and partnerships are all examples of this. Describe how the company intends to gain market share and differentiate itself in a crowded market.

- **Market risks and challenges:** Identify potential market risks and challenges that may have an impact on the business' success. This can include factors such as intense competition, changing consumer preferences, legal or regulatory barriers, or economic uncertainties. Discuss strategies for reducing these risks.

- **Future prospects:** This category includes all potential opportunities for growth and expansion within the target market. This could include adding new customer segments, expanding geographically, expanding product lines, or forming strategic alliances.

Strategy for Marketing and Sales

This strategy outlines the company's approach and tactics for promoting and selling its products or services to its target market. To achieve the required sales, it considers a variety of factors, such as the target market, marketing channels, pricing, and sales strategies. The following are the key components that must be addressed in this section of the business plan:

- **Target market:** Clearly define the specific market segments that the company intends to target. Describe the ideal customer's characteristics and why they are a good fit for the product or service. This aids in the customization of marketing efforts and messaging in order to effectively reach the target audience.

- **Positioning and messaging:** Determine the product's or service's unique value proposition and how it will be positioned in the market. The message must be compelling and communicate to the target audience the benefits, features, and differentiation. Highlight the reasons why customers should choose your company over competitors.

- **Marketing channels:** Determine which marketing channels will be used to reach your target market. This includes both online channels such as social media, search engine marketing, and email marketing, as well as traditional channels such as print advertising, television, and radio. The channels you select should address your target audience directly.

- **Marketing campaigns:** Outline the specific marketing campaigns and initiatives that will be implemented to promote the product or service. Product launches, content marketing, influence partnerships, events, and promotional activities are all examples of this. Set the timeline, budget, and expected outcomes for each campaign.

- **Price strategy:** Describe your pricing strategy for your product or service. Discuss the pricing model, pricing tiers (if applicable), and any other promotional pricing or discounts that will be available. When deciding on a price, consider your value proposition, your competitors' pricing, and what your target audience is willing to pay.

- **Sales strategy:** Describe in detail your intended sales approach and tactics. The entire sales process, from lead generation to lead qualification, nurturing, and closing techniques, should be covered. Determine the structure, roles, and responsibilities of the sales team, if applicable.

- **Distribution channels:** If your product or service requires distribution, describe the channels you will use. Direct sales, partnerships with retailers or distributors, and online marketplaces are all examples of this. Explain why the distribution channels were chosen and how they align with the target market.

- **Marketing budget:** Provide an overview of the marketing budget required to carry out the plans described in the marketing and sales strategy section. Outline any estimated costs for the various marketing activities you intend to undertake. Ensure that the budget does not exceed the company's financial resources or the expected return on investment.

- **Metrics of performance:** How will you assess the effectiveness of your marketing and sales efforts? Consider the cost of acquiring a customer, conversion rates, customer lifetime value, and return on marketing investment. Set specific targets and objectives for each metric.

- **Monitoring and evaluation:** Explain how marketing and sales strategies will be monitored and evaluated. Describe how you will collect the necessary data, analyze the results, and make data-driven changes to optimize marketing and sales activities.

Organizational Structure and Management

This section provides an overview of the company's structure, key personnel roles and responsibilities, and the qualifications of the management team. It describes the organization's hierarchy, reporting relationships, and decision-making processes. The key issues to address in the section are:

- **Organizational structure:** Describe the overall structure of the organization, including whether it is a sole proprietorship, partnership, corporation, or another legal entity. Outline the company's position and department hierarchy, demonstrating how they are organized and interact with one another.

- **Key personnel:** Identify the key people in your organization, such as the founders, owners, board members, and executive team. Give a summary of their qualifications, expertise, and relevant experience. Highlight their roles and responsibilities within the organization.

- **Management team:** Introduce the management team and highlight their combined experience and expertise. Include key positions like CEO, CFO, COO, and department heads. Describe their roles and how they contribute to the company's overall management and strategic direction.

- **Organizational chart:** Include an organizational chart to visually represent the company's reporting relationships and hierarchy. This diagram depicts the structure and roles of each department or team member, demonstrating how they are linked and to whom they report.

- **Responsibilities and roles:** Clearly outline the roles and responsibilities of key personnel and department heads. Describe their areas of expertise and the functions they oversee. This helps to provide clarity on who is responsible for what within the organization.

- **Advisory board or board or directors:** If applicable, mention the presence of an advisory board or board of directors. Describe their roles, qualifications, and how they contribute to the strategic decision-making process.

- **Management philosophy:** In short discuss the management philosophy or approach that guides the organization. This can include values, principles, or a particular management style that the company follows.

- **Succession planning:** What are the succession plans within the management team or key positions? Give an outline of how the company will handle leadership transitions and ensure continuity in the event of key personnel changes.

- **Staffing and human resources:** Provide an overview of the company's approach to staffing and human resources management. Discuss recruitment strategies, employee training and development programs, and any unique approaches to fostering a positive work culture.

- **Legal and compliance considerations:** Mention any legal and compliance considerations related to the organizational structure and management. This may include licenses, permits, certifications, or industry-specific regulations that need to be adhered to.

Financial Projections

This section forecasts the company's financial performance over a specific time period, typically three to five years. It includes estimates for revenue, expenses, and profitability, as well as projections for key financial indicators. Key components for this section include:

- **Revenue projections:** Estimate the company's expected revenue sources and forecast sales figures for each product or service category. Market research, historical data, industry trends, and anticipated customer demand can all be used to make this decision.

- **COGS (cost of goods sold):** Determine the direct costs of producing and/or delivering the company's products or services. This includes costs such as raw materials, labor, and manufacturing overhead. Estimate the COGS based on expected sales volumes and manufacturing costs.

- **Operating expenses:** Outline the expected operating expenses for the business. Rent, utilities, salaries and wages, marketing expenses, insurance, and administrative costs are all included. Calculate these costs using historical data, market research, and industry benchmarks.

- **Gross margin:** Determine the gross margin by subtracting the COGS from the projected revenue. This represents the company's profitability before operational expenses, interest, taxes, and other non-operating expenses are deducted.

- **Net income:** Income calculated by subtracting interest expenses, taxes, and other non-operating expenses from operating income. This is the total profit after all expenses are deducted.

- **Cash flow projections:** Focuses on estimates for cash inflows and outflows, including cash from sales, loans, investments, and operating activities, as well as cash outflows for expenses, investments, and debt repayment. This will aid in determining the company's ability to generate and manage cash efficiently.

- **Financial ratios:** Determine important financial ratios such as gross margin ratio, net profit margin, return on investment (ROI), and break even analysis. These ratios provide information about the profitability, efficiency, and financial health of the company.

- **Assumptions and justifications:** Document the assumptions and justifications used to develop the financial projections. Explain why the estimates were made, including market trends, competitive analysis, pricing strategies, and cost-cutting measures.

- **Sensitivity analysis:** Perform a sensitivity analysis to determine the impact of changes in key variables on financial projections. This assists in identifying the most critical factors that may impact the company's financial performance and enables scenario planning.

Funding Requirements

A business plan's funding requirements description outlines the company's financial needs and provides an overview of the funding required to support the company's operations and growth. It specifies the amount of capital required, as well as the purpose of the funds and how they will be used. The following are the most critical elements to include:

- **Capital expenditures:** Determine the specific capital outlays required to start or expand the business. Costs for equipment, machinery, vehicles, technology infrastructure, and any other long-term assets required for operations are included.

- **Working capital:** Determine the amount of working capital required to cover day-to-day operational expenses such as inventory, raw materials, salaries, rent, utilities, marketing, and other ongoing costs. Working capital ensures that the business has enough liquidity to run its daily operations.

- **Research and development:** If applicable, outline any research and development (R&D) costs necessary to develop new products, improve existing products, or explore new markets. R&D funding may be required for activities like market research, product testing, prototype development, or intellectual property protection.

- **Marketing and advertising:** Determine the budget needed for marketing and advertising initiatives to promote the company's products and services. Advertising campaigns, digital marketing efforts, social media promotions, trade shows, and other marketing strategies are all included.

- **Expansion and growth:** Specify the funding required for these initiatives if the company intends to expand its operations or enter new markets. This could include the costs of opening new locations, entering new markets, hiring more employees, or implementing new technologies.

- **Debt repayment:** If the business has existing debt obligations, outline any funds required for debt repayment. This includes loan installments, interest payments, or other debt obligations that need to be fulfilled.

- **Contingency fund:** It might be prudent to include a contingency fund to provide for any unexpected expenses or fluctuations in the business environment. A contingency fund acts as a buffer to handle unforeseen circumstances or challenges that may arise.

- **Funding sources:** Identify the potential sources of funding to meet the company's financial requirements. This may include equity financing (like investments from founders, partners, or investors), debt financing (like bank loans or other lines of credit), government grants or subsidies, or other financing options.

- **Timeline and milestones:** Provide a timeline indicating when the funding will be required, as well as any significant funding milestones. This helps to align the funding requirements with the operational and growth plans of the company.

- **Financial projections:** Link the funding needs to the financial projections in each section. Demonstrate how the funds will help the company's growth, revenue generation, and profitability. This provides a clear explanation for the requested funding.

Risk Analysis and Mitigation

This section outlines the potential risks and uncertainties that could jeopardize the company's success and proposes strategies for managing and mitigating those risks. It entails identifying, assessing, and mitigating various risks in order to reduce their impact on the company's operations, financial performance, and overall health. This section's key components are as follows:

- **Risk identification:** Entails identifying and categorizing potential risks that the company may face. Market risks (such as changes in customer behavior or competition), operational risks (such as supply chain disruptions or technological challenges), financial risks (such as cash flow challenges or economic downturns), and legal and regulatory risks (such as compliance issues or changes in legislation) are examples of these risks.

- **Risk assessment:** The likelihood and potential impact of each identified risk on the business are considered in risk assessment. Examine the likelihood of occurrence as well as the potential consequences for the company's financial health, reputation, operations, and strategic goals. This helps prioritize risks based on their importance and allows for more targeted mitigation efforts.

- **Mitigation strategies:** Create strategies and action plans to manage and mitigate the risks that have been identified. These strategies can include both preventative measures to reduce the likelihood of risks occurring and contingency plans to address risks if they do occur. Diversifying the customer base, implementing robust operational and financial controls, securing insurance coverage, conducting thorough due diligence, or seeking legal counsel are all examples of mitigation strategies.

- **Risk monitoring:** Entails establishing a system to continuously monitor and track the identified risks. Review the effectiveness of risk mitigation strategies on a regular basis and assess any changes in the risk landscape. This enables proactive adjustments and the addition of additional measures as required.

- **Contingency planning:** The preparation for critical risks that could have a significant impact on the business. These plans outline alternative courses of action to be taken if specific risks materialize. Contingency planning ensures that the company is ready to respond to unforeseen events quickly and effectively.

- **Business continuity:** Concerned with the continuation of operations in the face of potential threats. Identify critical business functions, assets, and resources, and create plans to ensure their continued operation or rapid recovery in the event of a disruption.

- **Documentation and review:** Refers to the process of reviewing and updating risk analysis and mitigation strategies as the company grows. This demonstrates a proactive risk management approach and demonstrates that the company is responsive to changes in the business environment.

Implementation Plan

This section outlines the specific steps and actions that will be taken to carry out the strategies and initiatives outlined in the plan. It serves as a road map for transforming the business plan into actionable tasks and ensures a systematic approach to meeting the company's goals and objectives. This section should include the following elements:

- **Next steps:** Divide the overall business plan into manageable steps and tasks. Determine the key activities, milestones, and deliverables that must be completed in order to carry out the strategies outlined in the plan. Each section should be specific, measurable, achievable, relevant, and time-bound (SMART) (Leonard & Watts, 2021).

- **Responsible parties:** Individuals or teams should be assigned responsibility for each action step. Define who will be held accountable for completing tasks and meeting objectives. This ensures that everyone involved in the implementation process understands their roles and responsibilities.

- **Timeline:** Create a timeline for each step's implementation. Set reasonable completion dates for tasks and milestones. The timeline provides a structured approach and aids in tracking progress, ensuring that activities are completed on time.

- **Allocation of resources:** Determine the resources needed to effectively implement the plan. Human resources, financial resources, technology, equipment, and any other assets required are all included. Set aside resources to help with the execution of the action steps.

- **Budgeting:** Create a budget outlining the financial requirements for carrying out the plan. Determine the costs associated with each action step, taking into account factors such as personnel costs, marketing expenses, technology investments, and operational expenses. Ensure that adequate funding is set aside to support the implementation efforts.

- **Communication and collaboration:** Create effective communication channels and mechanisms for team members and stakeholders to collaborate. To ensure alignment and engagement throughout the implementation process, communicate progress updates on a regular basis, share relevant information, and foster a collaborative environment.

- **Monitoring and evaluation:** Set up a monitoring and evaluation system to track the implementation plan's progress. Create metrics to assess the effectiveness of each action step. Review and evaluate these outcomes on a regular basis, making adjustments as needed to stay on track and addressing challenges as they arise.

- **Contingency planning:** Prepare for potential challenges or risks that may arise during the implementation process. Create contingency plans or alternative action plans to deal with unexpected situations. This ensures that the implementation plan remains adaptable and flexible in the face of changing circumstances.

- **Review and update:** As the business grows, the implementation plan should be reviewed and updated on a regular basis. Evaluate the effectiveness of the actions taken and make adjustments as needed to keep up with changing needs or market conditions.

Appendix

The appendix is a section that contains supplementary materials, documents, or data that support and expand on the information presented in the plan's main body. While the main sections of the business plan concentrate on important aspects such as the executive summary, company description, market analysis, and financial projections, the appendix holds additional information that may be useful or necessary for stakeholders to review. Common items that may be included in the appendix are:

- **Supporting documents:** This can include copies of legal documents, licenses, permits, contracts, patents, or any other legal or regulatory paperwork that is important for the business.

- **Market research data:** Market research reports, surveys, or studies that provide additional insights into the target market, customer demographics, industry trends, and competitive analysis.

- **Financial statements:** Detailed financial statements like balance sheets, income statements, and cash flow statements. These statements provide a comprehensive view of the company's financial performance and help validate the projections and assumptions made in the business plan.

- **Employee information:** Resumes and biographies for key team members, executives, or founders that highlight their qualifications, experience, and expertise; this data helps to demonstrate the capabilities and credibility of the business's team.

- **Product brochures or samples:** Marketing materials, product brochures, or samples that highlight the company's products or services. These materials can provide a tangible representation of the offerings while also supporting the descriptions provided in the business plan's major sections.

- **Letters of support or recommendation:** Letters from clients, partners, or industry experts confirming the business concept, market potential, and company capabilities. These letters lend credibility to the business idea and demonstrate external validation.

- **A list of references or sources:** This is used to gather market research data or industry information and is referred to as a market research sources list. This helps stakeholders verify the credibility of the research and gain further insights if needed.

- **Other relevant information:** This can include product specifications, legal disclaimers, detailed marketing plans, organizational charts, or any other pertinent materials.

Example of a Basic Business Plan

This business plan is written for a fictional business specializing in cleaning carpet and upholstery and will be presented to a possible investor.

Welcome to Cleanworx, your reliable partner for professional carpet and upholstery cleaning services. We at Cleanworx understand how important it is to have a clean and healthy environment in which to live or work. Our mission is to provide exceptional cleaning solutions to restore the beauty and freshness of your carpets and upholstery.

Cleanworx has a long history of excellence and customer satisfaction. We are a family-owned company committed to providing high-quality cleaning services tailored to your specific requirements. Our trained technicians use advanced cleaning techniques and environmentally friendly products to achieve outstanding results while putting our customers' health and safety first.

In this business plan, we will give you a comprehensive overview of Cleanworx and our success strategies. We will look at market research, marketing and sales strategies, organizational structure, financial projections, and other topics. Our dedication to exceptional service, attention to detail, and customer satisfaction distinguishes Cleanworx as a leader in the carpet and upholstery cleaning industry.

Thank you for taking the time to consider Cleanworx for your cleaning needs. We are excited to serve you and provide a clean and refreshed environment that exceeds your expectations.

Executive Summary

Cleanworx is a professional cleaning services company that specializes in carpet and upholstery cleaning. Our mission is to provide both residential and commercial customers with high-quality and dependable cleaning solutions. Cleanworx aims to establish itself as a leading provider of carpet and upholstery cleaning services in the local market by focusing on customer satisfaction and delivering exceptional results.

At Cleanworx, we understand the importance of a clean and healthy environment in improving people's overall well-being and extending the life of carpets and upholstery. We guarantee professional service that restores the beauty and freshness of your carpets and upholstery with our team of experienced and well-trained technicians.

We ensure thorough cleaning without jeopardizing our customers' health and safety by employing advanced cleaning techniques and eco-friendly products. Our deep carpet cleaning, stain removal, and upholstery cleaning services are tailored to each client's specific requirements. We also provide odor removal as well as Scotchgard® protection for your carpets and upholstery.

Cleanworx is well-positioned to benefit from the rising demand for professional cleaning services. Our target market includes both residential customers seeking periodic cleaning for their homes and commercial clients such as offices, hotels, and healthcare facilities that require consistent and dependable cleaning solutions.

We recognize the significance of effective marketing and sales strategies in reaching and attracting our target audience. We hope to increase brand visibility and generate a steady stream of loyal customers through online marketing, local advertising, strategic partnerships, and excellent customer service. Our commitment to customer satisfaction and personalized recommendations ensure that our clients receive the best cleaning solutions possible, tailored to their specific requirements.

Cleanworx is dedicated to delivering exceptional results and has a strong organizational structure and management team. Our founder and owner work closely with our skilled technicians to provide dependable and efficient cleaning services that consistently meet and exceed customer expectations.

Cleanworx is looking for funding primarily through personal investment and a small business loan. These funds will be used to acquire professional-grade cleaning equipment, implement effective marketing and advertising campaigns, secure funds for possible expansions, and cover unexpected operational expenses.

While every business faces risks, we have put measures in place to mitigate these risks and ensure smooth operations. We adapt and thrive in a competitive industry thanks to our ongoing monitoring of market trends, competitive pricing, exceptional service quality, and customer feedback.

The implementation plan outlines our strategy for launching and growing Cleanworx, including infrastructure development, procurement of equipment and supplies, hiring and training staff, development of marketing materials, and execution of marketing and sales strategies. We will be able to achieve our goals and establish Cleanworx as the go-to choice for carpet and upholstery cleaning services if we regularly monitor and evaluate our strategies.

Company Description

Cleanworx is a family-owned business specializing in professional carpet and upholstery cleaning services. As a limited liability company (LLC) registered under the name Cleanworx Cleaning Services, LLC, we are committed to providing exceptional cleaning solutions to our valued customers. Our mission is to deliver top-quality cleaning services that transform spaces into clean, fresh, and healthy environments. We envision becoming the leading provider of carpet and upholstery cleaning services in our region, recognized for our commitment to customer satisfaction and environmentally friendly practices.

Founded in 2005 by John and Emily Johnson, Cleanworx has grown from a small operation to a reputable cleaning services provider. With over 15 years of industry experience, John and Emily bring a wealth of knowledge and expertise to the company. As co-founders and owners, they oversee the day-to-day operations and ensure the highest standards of service delivery.

Our target market includes homeowners, renters, and businesses in our local area who value cleanliness and seek professional cleaning services. We cater to a wide range of clients, including residential properties, offices, hotels, restaurants, and healthcare facilities. By understanding the specific needs of each client segment, we can deliver personalized cleaning solutions that exceed their expectations.

Cleanworx differentiates itself from competitors through our commitment to eco-friendly practices. We understand the importance of minimizing our environmental impact while still delivering outstanding results. Our use of safe and non-toxic cleaning products ensures the well-being of our customers, their families, and the environment.

Located in the heart of our community, Cleanworx operates from our facility at 123 Main Street, providing us with easy access to serve our target market efficiently. We comply with all legal and regulatory requirements related to business licensing, insurance, and environmental regulations, ensuring that our operations are conducted responsibly and ethically.

Products and Services

Cleanworx provides a full range of professional carpet and upholstery cleaning services. Our mission is to provide outstanding cleaning solutions that leave our customers' spaces looking fresh, clean, and revitalized. Here is a summary of our main services:

Deep Carpet Cleaning

Our deep carpet cleaning service removes embedded dirt, stains, and allergens from carpets using advanced techniques and cutting-edge equipment. To ensure a thorough and safe cleaning process, we use hot water extraction methods and eco-friendly cleaning solutions.

Upholstery Cleaning

Our upholstery cleaning service specializes in revitalizing and restoring the appearance of furniture such as sofas, chairs, and ottomans. We use specialized cleaning agents and techniques to effectively remove dirt, dust, and stains from upholstery fabrics, leaving them clean and fresh.

Key Features:

- Professional and thorough cleaning methods

- Using eco-friendly cleaning products

- Technicians with training and experience

- Detail and precision in the cleaning process

Benefits:

- Removal of dirt, stains, and allergens, improving space cleanliness and hygiene

- Restoring the appearance and freshness of carpets and upholstery

- Elimination of odors, resulting in a more inviting environment

- Carpet and upholstery lifespan is extended, reducing the need for frequent replacements.

Value Proposition

Cleanworx distinguishes itself by its dedication to providing exceptional cleaning services. To achieve outstanding results, we prioritize customer satisfaction by utilizing advanced cleaning techniques and eco-friendly products. Our attention to detail, professionalism, and commitment to meeting the needs of our customers set us apart from the competition.

Pricing

Our pricing structure is competitive and tailored to each project's specific needs. To provide accurate and fair pricing, factors such as the size of the area, the condition of the carpets or upholstery, and any additional treatments required are considered.

Intellectual Property

Cleanworx currently does not own any intellectual property related to our cleaning services. However, in order to maintain our expertise and deliver exceptional results, we continually invest in training and stay up to date with the latest industry best practices.

Development and Production

Our cleaning services adhere to industry best practices and methods. We are constantly evaluating and implementing new cleaning technologies and products that are environmentally friendly and provide superior cleaning results.

Life Cycle

Our services' life cycle includes several stages, including customer consultation, pre-cleaning assessment, actual cleaning process, and post-cleaning inspection. We strive to build long-term relationships with our customers by providing ongoing maintenance and periodic cleaning as needed.

Competitive Analysis

Cleanworx competes in the market with other local cleaning service providers. Our dedication to exceptional service, eco-friendly practices, and customer satisfaction, on the other hand, distinguishes us. To stay ahead of the competition and improve our services, we constantly monitor market trends and customer feedback.

Future Opportunities

Cleanworx sees several future opportunities for growth as the demand for professional cleaning services grows. These include expanding our customer base to new market segments, diversifying our service offerings to include additional cleaning solutions, and exploring partnerships with complementary businesses to enhance our service offerings.

Market Research

Industry Overview

The demand for professional cleaning services in both residential and commercial settings has driven consistent growth in the carpet and upholstery cleaning industry over the years. As people and businesses prioritize cleanliness and hygiene, the demand for specialized cleaning solutions has grown. The industry is distinguished by the presence of both small local cleaning service providers and larger national corporations.

Target Market

Cleanworx primarily serves residential and commercial clients within a 50-mile radius of our office. Our services cater to homeowners, rental property owners, office spaces, retail establishments, and hospitality businesses. By focusing on both residential and commercial markets, we can maximize our customer base and revenue potential.

Market Size and Growth

The carpet and upholstery cleaning market in our target area is estimated to be worth $X million annually, and it has been growing at an average rate of $X\%$ over the past few years. This growth can be attributed to increased awareness of the benefits of professional cleaning, changing consumer preferences, and the expansion of commercial spaces.

Market Trends

- Growing preference for eco-friendly cleaning solutions and practices
- Increased demand for specialized stain and odor removal services
- Rising popularity of maintenance contracts and recurring cleaning services
- Adoption of advanced cleaning technologies and equipment

- Shift toward online booking platforms for convenient service scheduling

Customer Analysis

Our target customers are individuals and businesses that value cleanliness, hygiene, and the preservation of their carpets and upholstery. Residential customers include homeowners, renters, and property managers seeking professional cleaning services to maintain the appearance and cleanliness of their homes. Commercial customers encompass businesses in various sectors, such as offices, hotels, restaurants, and retail establishments, where cleanliness and aesthetics are critical for creating a positive impression on customers.

Unique Selling Propositions

- Use of eco-friendly cleaning products and practices, appealing to environmentally conscious customers

- Attention to detail and commitment to delivering exceptional cleaning results

- Trained and experienced technicians ensuring a professional and efficient service

- Customized cleaning solutions tailored to the specific needs of each customer

Market Entry Strategy

Cleanworx will employ a multi-channel marketing approach to establish a strong presence in the market. This will include a combination of online marketing, such as a professional website and social media presence, targeted local advertising, partnerships with real estate agencies and property management companies, and networking within the local business community.

Market Risks and Challenges

- Intense competition from existing service providers in the area

- Economic downturn affecting discretionary spending on cleaning services

- Reputation management and addressing customer concerns effectively

- Adapting to evolving customer preferences and market trends

Future Prospects

The future prospects for Cleanworx are promising. As the demand for professional cleaning services continues to rise, we anticipate steady growth and expansion. By consistently delivering exceptional service, nurturing customer relationships, and staying ahead of market trends, we aim to position Cleanworx as a trusted and preferred provider of carpet and upholstery cleaning services in our target market.

Strategy for Marketing and Sales

Target Market

Cleanworx focuses on reaching residential and commercial customers within a 50-mile radius of our business location. By understanding their needs and preferences, we can tailor our marketing and sales efforts to effectively target and engage our desired customer base.

Positioning and Messaging

Cleanworx positions itself as a trusted provider of professional and eco-friendly carpet and upholstery cleaning services. Our messaging emphasized our commitment to delivering exceptional results, using safe and sustainable cleaning practices, and providing personalized solutions that meet our customers' specific cleaning requirements.

Marketing Channels

Cleanworx will run targeted marketing campaigns throughout the year to generate brand awareness and attract new customers. These campaigns will highlight our unique selling propositions, special offers, and the benefits of professional cleaning. We will also offer referral programs to incentivize existing customers to refer our services to their friends and family.

Pricing Strategy

Our pricing strategy will be competitive, taking into consideration factors such as the size of the area to be cleaned, the difficulty of the job, and any additional services requested. We will provide clear cost breakdowns and transparent pricing to ensure customers understand the value they receive for their investment in our services.

Sales Strategy

Cleanworx will prioritize developing strong customer relationships and providing exceptional customer service. Our sales representatives will be trained to provide detailed information about our services, respond to customer inquiries, and provide accurate and competitive quotes. We will highlight the advantages of professional cleaning as well as the long-term value it provides to the customer.

Distribution Channels

Cleanworx is a service-based company that does not rely on traditional distribution channels. Instead, we will deliver our services directly to the customer's location. We will ensure that scheduling and coordination are efficient in order to meet customer demands and provide a seamless and convenient experience.

Marketing Budget

Cleanworx has set aside a marketing budget to supplement our marketing and sales efforts. This budget will cover advertising costs both online and offline, promotional materials, website maintenance, and marketing campaigns. The budget will be reviewed and adjusted on a regular basis based on the performance and effectiveness of various marketing channels.

Metrics of Performance, Monitoring, and Evaluation

Cleanworx will track key performance indicators such as customer acquisition rate, conversion rate, customer satisfaction, and revenue growth to assess the success of our marketing and sales efforts. We will monitor and evaluate the effectiveness of our marketing campaigns, marketing channels, and sales strategies using analytical tools and customer feedback. Regular assessments will help us make data-driven decisions to improve our marketing and sales strategies.

Organizational Structure and Management

Organizational Structure

Cleanworx employs a hierarchical organizational structure to ensure efficient management and operation coordination. The structure is made up of various departments and positions that collaborate to provide high-quality carpet and upholstery cleaning services.

Key Personnel

John and Sarah Thompson, the company's founders, have a lot of experience in the cleaning industry. They set the company's strategic direction and created key divisions to drive growth and success. The management team also includes experienced professionals in operations, marketing, finance, and customer service.

Management Team

Cleanworx's management team is made up of experts in their respective fields. A general manager is in charge of overall operations; a marketing manager is in charge of marketing campaigns and customer acquisition; a finance manager is in charge of financial management and budgeting; and a customer service manager is in charge of providing excellent customer service.

Responsibilities and Roles

Each position at Cleanworx has well-defined responsibilities and roles. Everyone understands their specific duties and contributes to the smooth operation of the company, from technicians who provide cleaning services to managers who oversee various aspects of the business.

Advisory Board or Board of Directors

Cleanworx has a board of advisors made up of industry experts and professionals who provide valuable guidance and strategic advice. Their combined knowledge helps with decision-making, market insights, and overall business growth.

Management Philosophy

Cleanworx follows a management philosophy that emphasizes professionalism, integrity, and continuous improvement. The company places a premium on open communication, teamwork, and a customer-focused approach. Decisions are made based on data-driven insights and consideration for the long-term sustainability of the business.

Succession Planning

Cleanworx recognizes the importance of succession planning in maintaining business continuity and smooth leadership transitions. The organization has implemented a comprehensive succession plan to identify and develop talented employees for future leadership positions.

Staffing and Human Resources

Cleanworx is dedicated to hiring and retaining talented and dedicated employees. To attract qualified candidates, the company employs a thorough recruitment process and offers ongoing training and development opportunities to help them improve their skills and knowledge. Human resources policies and procedures are in place to foster a positive working environment and ensure employee satisfaction and productivity.

Legal and Compliance Considerations

In the carpet and upholstery cleaning industry, the company complies with all applicable legal and regulatory requirements. Safety standards, environmental regulations, and licensing requirements are all followed by the company. Cleanworx also keeps adequate insurance coverage in place to protect business stakeholders.

Financial Projections

Revenue Projections

Cleanworx expects consistent revenue growth over the next three years, owing to rising market demand for high-quality carpet and upholstery cleaning services. We anticipate revenue of $500,000 in the first year, $700,000 in the second year, and $900,000 in the third year, based on market research and historical data.

Cost of Goods Sold (COGS)

Cleanworx's COGS include direct labor costs, cleaning supplies, and equipment maintenance costs that are directly related to service delivery. We estimate COGS to be around 40% of total revenue, allowing for a 60% gross margin.

Gross Margin and Net Income

We anticipate a strong net income for Cleanworx with a gross margin of 60% and operating expenses factored in. We expect a $100,000 net profit in the first year, $150,000 in the second year, and $200,000 in the third year.

Cash Flow Projections

Cleanworx has created detailed cash flow projections to ensure adequate liquidity for day-to-day operations, equipment upgrades, and future growth. We anticipate positive cash flow throughout the projection period by carefully managing receivables and payables.

Financial Ratios

To evaluate its financial health and performance, the company closely monitors key financial ratios. These ratios include liquidity ratios (current and quick ratio), profitability ratios (gross and net profit margin), and efficiency ratios (asset and receivables turnover). It is critical to maintain healthy financial ratios in order to sustain profitability and secure potential financing options.

Assumptions and Justifications

Our financial projections are based on several key assumptions, including market growth rates, customer acquisition rates, pricing strategies, and operational efficiencies. These assumptions have been carefully justified using industry research, competitor analysis, and historical data.

Sensitivity Analysis

The company has performed a sensitivity analysis to determine the impact of external factors on financial projections. This analysis evaluates the company's resilience and adaptability to changing market conditions by taking into account scenarios such as changes in market demand, price fluctuations, and cost variations.

Funding Requirements

Capital Expenditures

Cleanworx's funding requirements to support its business operations and growth initiatives are as follows:

Working Capital

The company requires working capital to cover expenses such as payroll, supplies, and overhead costs in order to run smoothly on a daily basis. We estimate that $50,000 in working capital will be required to sustain operations in the first few months before achieving positive cash flow.

Research and Development

Cleanworx recognizes the importance of innovation and staying ahead of market trends. We have allocated $20,000 for R&D initiatives, including the exploration of eco-friendly cleaning solutions and the development of new cleaning techniques.

Marketing and Advertising

To establish brand awareness, attract new customers, and capture a significant market share, Cleanworx plans to allocate $30,000 for marketing and advertising campaigns. These initiatives will include digital marketing, social media advertising, local promotions, and strategic partnerships.

Expansion and Growth

As the company's customer base and operations grow, it plans to open additional service locations in nearby cities. The cost of expansion and growth initiatives is estimated to be $150,000, which includes securing new leases, hiring additional staff, and investing in marketing efforts in target markets.

Debt Repayment

Cleanworx intends to use some of its funds to pay off any initial loans or debts incurred during the startup phase. By prioritizing debt repayment, the company's financial position will be strengthened, and future finance expenses will be reduced.

Contingency Fund

The company understands the value of having a contingency fund to deal with unforeseen circumstances or business challenges. We have set aside $20,000 as a contingency reserve to ensure financial stability and flexibility in the event of an unexpected event.

Funding Resources

Cleanworx intends to seek funding from a variety of sources, including equity investments, business loans, and potentially available grants or subsidies for environmentally friendly businesses. The company/s founders will also put up their own money to help with the startup phase.

Timeline and Milestones

The company intends to secure the necessary funding within the next six months in order to begin operations and implement its growth plans. The funding timeline corresponds to the company's strategic milestones, such as equipment procurement, staff recruitment, and the launch of marketing campaigns.

Financial Projections

Cleanworx's funding requirements correspond to the company's financial projections, which demonstrate the company's ability to generate positive cash flow, achieve profitability, and provide a return on investment to potential funders. The financial projections lay out a clear path for long-term growth and financial success.

Risk Analysis and Mitigation

Cleanworx has conducted an extensive risk analysis to identify potential risks and challenges that could affect its operations and financial performance. The following are the key risks identified:

Competitive Risk

The carpet and upholstery cleaning industry is highly competitive. Cleanworx will mitigate this risk by distinguishing itself through exceptional customer service, competitive pricing, and an emphasis on environmentally friendly cleaning practices. Cleanworx will be able to adapt its strategies as a result of regular market research and competitor monitoring.

Economic Risk

Economic fluctuations can have an impact on consumer spending habits, which could affect demand for cleaning services. To mitigate the impact of economic downturns, Cleanworx will closely monitor economic indicators and diversify its customer base. Cleanworx aims to be resilient in various economic conditions by providing high-quality services at competitive prices.

Operational Risk

Cleanworx's success depends on efficient operations. The company will put in place strict quality control measures, invest in regular equipment maintenance, and provide extensive training to its employees. Furthermore, having contingency plans in place for unforeseen circumstances such as equipment breakdowns or staff shortages will ensure that services are disrupted as little as possible.

Regulatory and Compliance Risk

Cleanworx works in a highly regulated industry with strict guidelines for environmental standards and cleaning agent disposal. The company will comply with all applicable regulations, obtain all necessary licenses and permits, and use environmentally-friendly practices. Internal audits will be conducted on a regular basis to ensure compliance with all regulatory requirements.

Health and Safety Risk

Cleanworx prioritizes the health and safety of its employees and customers. The company will implement comprehensive safety protocols, provide appropriate training, and ensure compliance with occupational health and safety regulations. To reduce the risk of accidents or injuries, equipment will be inspected and maintained on a regular basis.

Mitigation Strategies

To address these identified risks, Cleanworx has developed a number of mitigation strategies. These include:

- Developing strong customer relationships and loyalty through high-quality service and personalized experiences.

- Maintaining a diverse customer base across residential, commercial, and industrial sectors to mitigate the impact of changes in market demand.

- Creating strong supplier relationships to ensure a consistent supply of cleaning supplies and equipment.

- Investing in technology and automation to improve operational efficiency and streamline operations.

- Keeping comprehensive insurance coverage in place to reduce financial risks associated with potential liabilities.

- Regular skill development programs are run to improve employee capabilities and overall service quality.

Risk Monitoring and Contingency Planning

Cleanworx will implement a risk monitoring system to assess and reassess potential risks on a regular basis. This will entail conducting periodic risk assessments, monitoring industry trends, and soliciting customer feedback. Contingency plans will be developed for each identified risk to ensure an effective response and resolution if it occurs.

Business Continuity

Cleanworx understands the value of business continuity in the face of unforeseen events. During disruptions such as natural disasters, equipment failures, or workforce issues, the company will establish protocols to ensure the smooth continuation of operations. Critical data and documents will be synced to a cloud storage application, and as part of the contingency planning process, alternative service providers or suppliers will be identified.

Documentation and Review

Cleanworx will keep detailed records of risk analysis, mitigation strategies, and contingency plans. These documents will be reviewed and updated on a regular basis to ensure their effectiveness in addressing changing risks and industry dynamics. Cleanworx will also conduct internal and external audits on a regular basis to assess the implementation and effectiveness of risk management practices.

Implementation Plan

Cleanworx has created a comprehensive implementation plan to ensure that its strategies are carried out smoothly and that its business objectives are met. The following sections outline the plan's key components:

Next Steps

Cleanworx will begin the implementation plan by identifying the immediate next steps needed to launch and grow the company. These steps include finalizing legal and licensing requirements, obtaining required permits, forming supplier partnerships, and hiring and training the initial workforce.

Responsible Parties

Specific tasks and responsibilities will be assigned to key individuals within the organization to ensure clear accountability. The implementation process will be overseen by the management team, and each team member will be responsible for completing their assigned tasks within the timeframes specified.

Timeline

Cleanworx has created a detailed timeline that outlines the major milestones and deadlines for various implementation activities. This timeline will serve as a roadmap for the team to track progress and ensure that each stage is completed on time.

Allocation of Resources

Cleanworx will allocate the resources required to support the implementation plan, including financial, human, and technological resources. Budgeting for equipment, supplies, marketing efforts, training programs, and any other resources needed for efficient operations is included.

Budgeting

A comprehensive budget will be created to outline the financial aspects of the implementation plan. Estimated costs, revenue projections, cash flow analysis, and ensuring adequate funds are allocated to various activities and initiatives are all part of this.

Communication and Collaboration

Effective communication and collaboration are critical for implementation success. Cleanworx will establish clear communication channels and protocols to ensure that team members' information flows smoothly. Team meetings, progress updates, and feedback sessions on a regular basis will promote cooperation and consistency.

Monitoring and Evaluation

Cleanworx recognizes the importance of monitoring and evaluating the progress and outcomes of the implementation plan. To evaluate the effectiveness of various strategies and initiatives, key performance indicators (KPIs) will be identified. As a result of regular monitoring, the management team will be able to make informed decisions, identify areas for improvement, and implement corrective actions as needed.

Contingency Planning

Cleanworx is aware of the potential difficulties and unexpected circumstances that may arise during implementation. To address these challenges, contingency plans will be developed, ensuring that alternative approaches and backup solutions are in place to minimize disruptions to operations.

Review and Update

The company recognizes the changing nature of the business environment and the importance of continuous improvement. The implementation plan will be reviewed and updated on a regular basis to adapt to market changes, incorporate feedback, and seize new opportunities. Cleanworx will be able to remain agile and responsive to emerging trends as a result of this continuous process.

Cleanworx hopes to effectively execute its strategies, meet established timelines, allocate resources efficiently, foster collaboration, monitor progress, and adapt to any unforeseen circumstances by adhering to the implementation plan. This will lay the groundwork for the company's successful launch and growth.

Conclusion

Finally, Cleanworx has created a detailed business plan outlining its vision, strategies, and implementation strategy for success in the carpet and upholstery cleaning industry. Cleanworx has established itself as a leading provider of high-quality, eco-friendly cleaning services through diligent research, careful analysis, and strategic planning.

The company's thorough market research identified a target market with significant growth potential, and its competitive advantages stem from its dedication to exceptional customer service, cutting-edge technology, and environmentally-friendly practices. The experienced management team at Cleanworx brings expertise and a shared vision to the company's success.

Furthermore, Cleanworx's implementation plan outlines key steps, responsible parties, timelines, resource allocation, and monitoring mechanisms to ensure that its strategies are successfully implemented. To adapt to market dynamics and seize opportunities, the plan highlights effective communication, collaboration, and preparedness for unforeseen circumstances.

Cleanworx is confident in its ability to meet customer needs, outperform competitors, and achieve its mission of providing impeccable cleaning services that enhance the comfort and well-being of its customers' living spaces by implementing the strategies outlined above. Cleanworx is excited to embark on this adventure and hopes to make a positive impact on the industry.

Quiz

1. Which section of a business plan typically provides an overview of the company's products or services, target market, competitive analysis, and marketing strategies?

(A) Executive summary

(B) Company description

(C) Market analysis

(D) Marketing and sales strategy

2. What is the purpose of the financial projections section in a business plan?

(A) To outline the company's organizational structure and management team

(B) To provide an overview of the company's products and services

(C) To describe the market size and growth potential

(D) To forecast the company's future financial performance

3. Which component of a business plan focuses on identifying potential risks and developing strategies to mitigate them?

(A) Financial projections

(B) Funding requirements

(C) Risk analysis and mitigation

(D) Implementation plan

4. What is the purpose of the appendix in a business plan?

(A) To provide an overview of the company's financial projections

(B) To outline the company's marketing and sales strategies

(C) To include supporting documents and additional information

(D) To describe the company's organizational structure and management team

5. Which section of a business plan typically provides an overview of the company's mission and vision statements, founders and key personnel, and company history?

(A) Company description

(B) Market analysis

(C) Financial projections

(D) Implementation plan

6. Which component of a business budget refers to the projected income or revenue that the business expects to generate during a specific period?

(A) Fixed costs

(B) Variable costs

(C) Cash flow

(D) Estimated revenue

Chapter Takeaway

In conclusion, developing a well-crafted business plan is essential for non-financial managers looking to navigate the complex world of business. It serves as a roadmap, guiding you through the various stages of planning, execution, and evaluation. A business plan helps you clarify your goals, identify potential challenges, and outline strategies for success. By conducting thorough market research, assessing financial viability, and setting clear objectives, you can effectively position your business for growth and adapt to changing market conditions. Remember, a solid business plan not only communicates your vision and potential to stakeholders, but also provides you with a valuable tool for decision-making and resource allocation.

Segue to Next Chapter

As we conclude our discussion of business plans, we will now turn our attention to another critical component of effective financial management: budgets and forecasts. While a business plan establishes the strategic direction and goals, budgets and forecasts provide the financial framework to turn those dreams into reality. In the following chapter, we will delve into the world of financial planning, emphasizing the importance of developing accurate budgets, forecasting revenue and expenses, and tracking financial performance. You will be better equipped to make informed financial decisions, allocate resources efficiently, and track progress toward your business objectives if you understand budgeting and forecasting. So, let's proceed to harness the power of budgets and forecasts to propel your organization toward long-term growth and success.

Chapter 9:

Budgeting and Forecasting

Before getting into the main components, let's briefly explain the main purpose of budgeting as follows.

The primary purposes of budgeting include:

- **Prioritizing spending:** A budget helps a company identify its most important expenses and ensure that they are adequately funded before allocating resources to less critical items.

- **Managing cash flow:** By planning income and expenses, a company can anticipate cash flow fluctuations and make adjustments to maintain financial stability.

- **Monitoring performance:** A budget serves as a benchmark for evaluating actual financial results against planned results, enabling managers to identify areas where improvements are needed.

- **Supporting decision-making:** Budgets provide valuable information for making strategic decisions, such as launching new products/service, expanding operations, or investing in new assets.

Budgeting and Types of Budgets

Budgeting and forecasting are related financial processes that serve different purposes in an organization's financial planning. While they are interconnected, they are not the same. Here's a brief explanation of their differences:

Budgeting

- **Purpose:** Budgeting involves creating a detailed financial plan for a specific period (usually annually) to allocate resources, control costs, and set financial targets. It helps organizations prioritize spending, manage cash flow, and monitor financial performance.

- **Timeframe:** Budgeting is typically done on a short-term basis, covering a single financial year. However, some organizations may create budgets for shorter or longer periods, such as quarterly or biennial budgets.

- **Focus:** A budget focuses on setting financial goals and allocating resources to meet those goals. It outlines the planned income, expenses, and cash flows for the organization during the budget period.

- **Rigidity:** Once a budget is approved, it generally remains fixed for the entire budget period. While some organizations may make adjustments during the year, budgets are typically less flexible than forecasts.

Forecasting

- **Purpose:** Forecasting is the process of estimating future financial outcomes based on historical data, market research, and business trends. It helps organizations anticipate changes in the business environment, identify opportunities and risks, and make informed decisions.

- **Timeframe:** Forecasts can cover both short and long-term periods, ranging from a few months to several years. They are usually updated more frequently than budgets to account for changes in the business environment or performance.

- **Focus:** Forecasts concentrate on predicting future financial results, such as revenues, expenses, and cash flows. They help organizations assess the potential impact of various scenarios, such as changes in market conditions, customer demand, or production costs.

- **Flexibility:** Forecasts are inherently more flexible than budgets, as they can be easily updated to reflect new information or changes in assumptions. This adaptability enables organizations to respond more quickly to changing circumstances and adjust their strategies accordingly.

Budgeting focuses on setting financial goals and allocating resources, while forecasting involves predicting future financial outcomes based on available information. Both processes are essential for effective financial planning and decision-making within an organization.

The Basics of Budgeting

A business budget is a financial plan that outlines a company's estimated revenue, expenses, and cash flow over a specific time period. It assists businesses in effectively allocating resources, monitoring financial performance, and making informed decisions.

Before getting into the main components, let's briefly explain the main purpose of budgeting. The primary purposes of budgeting include:

- **Prioritizing spending:** A budget helps a company identify its most important expenses and ensure that they are adequately funded before allocating resources to less critical items.

- **Managing cash flow:** By planning income and expenses, a company can anticipate cash flow fluctuations and make adjustments to maintain financial stability.

- **Monitoring performance:** A budget serves as a benchmark for evaluating actual financial results against planned results, enabling managers to identify areas where improvements are needed.

- **Supporting decision-making:** Budgets provide valuable information for making strategic decisions, such as launching new products/service, expanding operations, or investing in new assets.

Revenue Expected

Estimated revenue is an important component of a business budget because it represents the expected income or sales that a company anticipates generating over a specific time period, such as a month, quarter, or year. It serves as the foundation for financial planning and decision-making within the organization. To determine estimated revenue, businesses typically consider several factors, including historical sales data, market research, industry trends, customer demand, and sales forecasts. Here are some key points to understand about estimated revenue:

- **Sales forecasts:** Businesses project sales using a variety of methods, including analyzing historical sales patterns, conducting market research, and taking into account factors that may influence customer demand. Forecasts can be made based on the existing customer base, new customer acquisition, product pricing, marketing efforts, and market conditions.

- **Revenue streams:** Companies frequently generate revenue from a variety of sources, such as product sales, service fees, subscriptions, licensing, or advertising.

- **Sales volume and price:** Estimating revenue requires taking into account both the volume of sales and the pricing of products or services. Forecasted sales volumes can be based on market demand, target customer base, and production capacity. Pricing strategies such as discounts, promotions, or premium pricing can also have an impact on revenue estimates.

- **Trends and seasonality:** Due to factors such as holidays, weather, or industry-specific patterns, many businesses experience seasonal fluctuations in sales and income. Recognizing and incorporating seasonal trends into revenue projections is critical for accurate budgeting.

- **Adaptability and frequent revisions:** Revenue estimates are subject to change as market conditions change. Income projections must be reviewed and updated on a regular basis in response to actual sales performance and changes in market dynamics.

Fixed Expenses

Fixed costs refer to expenses that do not vary with changes in production or sales volume. These costs remain relatively constant over a given period, regardless of the business' level of activity. Here are some key points to understand about fixed costs in a budget:

- As fixed costs are relatively predictable, it is easy to budget for them as they remain constant over a specific period.

- Fixed costs may be relatively inflexible in the short term, but businesses have the opportunity to control or negotiate them during contract renewals or by seeking cost-saving measures. For example, exploring alternative suppliers or renegotiating lease agreements may help reduce fixed costs over the long run.

- Fixed costs are important in determining a company's break-even point. Understanding this cost allows businesses to determine the minimum level of sales or production required to cover expenses and begin generating profits.

Variable Costs

Variable costs are an important component of a business budget because they refer to expenses that vary depending on the level of production or sales. Variable costs vary in direct proportion to the quantity of products or services produced, as opposed to fixed costs, which remain relatively constant. When creating a budget, keep the following factors in mind:

- Variable costs are directly related to the volume of sales produced. Variable costs rise as the company's output rises. In the same way, if production or sales fall, variable costs fall as well.

- Variable costs are more adaptable than fixed costs because they can be adjusted to reflect changes in production or sales levels. For example, if production must be reduced, variable costs such as raw materials and direct labor can be reduced.

- Variable costs have a direct impact on a company's profitability because they are directly related to sales revenue. It is critical to monitor and manage variable costs in order to maintain a healthy profit margin. Businesses can determine their contribution margin (the amount left after deducting variable costs) and assess the profitability of various products or services by analyzing the relationship between variable costs and sales revenue.

- Variable costs are an important part of cost-volume-profit (CVP) analysis, which assists businesses in understanding the relationship between costs, volume, and profitability. Businesses can make informed decisions about pricing, sales targets, and production levels by taking variable costs into account alongside fixed costs and selling prices.

One-time Expenses

One-time or non-recurring expenses are costs that occur infrequently or as isolated events within a given time period. Unlike ongoing expenses, which are incurred on a regular basis, one-time expenses are one-of-a-kind and do not typically recur in subsequent budget cycles.

Cash Flow

Cash flow is an important part of a business budget because it focuses on tracking and managing the movement of money in and out of the company. It entails tracking cash inflows and outflows to ensure that the company has sufficient funds to meet its financial obligations.

Budgeting for cash flow entails forecasting cash inflows and outflows over a specified time period. This projection assists businesses in planning for potential cash shortfalls or surpluses and making informed cash management decisions. Businesses can predict periods of positive or negative cash flow by comparing projected cash inflows and outflows and taking proactive measures to address them.

Types of Budgets for Businesses

There are a number of budgets a business can make use of. To determine the most suitable budget, the following factors should be taken into consideration:

- **Determine the company's specific goals and objectives:** Budgets can serve various functions, such as controlling expenses, managing cash flow, and planning investments.

- **Consider the size and complexity of the company:** Smaller businesses may prefer simpler budgets, whereas larger organizations with multiple departments and activities may necessitate more detailed and comprehensive budgets. For example, during my first job as an accountant in the Hospitality sector, a subsidiary of Sri Lanka's largest blue chip company at the time, the budgeting process was extremely complicated due to the various departments and the multiple factors that affected revenue, marketing expenses, and other expenses.

- **Learn about the industry and market dynamics in which your company operates:** Consider industry benchmarks, market trends, and competitive factors that may influence budgetary decisions.

- **Examine the company's financial situation, including its revenue streams, costs, and cash flow patterns:** This will assist in determining the specific areas of focus and budgeting requirements.

- **Consider the stage of a company's lifecycle:** Budgets for start-ups may prioritize cash flow management and growth initiatives, whereas budgets for more mature businesses may focus on cost optimization and profit maximization.

Operating Budget

The operating budget is a financial plan that outlines a company;s projected income, costs, and expenses for a specific time period, usually monthly, quarterly, or annually. It focuses on the day-to-day operations of the company and provides a comprehensive view of its financial performance.

The main purposes of an operating budget are:

- **It helps set financial targets and establish benchmarks for the business' performance.** The budget lays out a strategy for meeting revenue and profit targets.

- **The operating budget assists in allocating resources effectively by identifying the expected costs and expenses.** It ensures that resources are directed toward areas that contribute to revenue generation and are in line with the company's strategic goals.

- **The budget helps to control costs by estimating and tracking operating expenses.** It enables businesses to track spending patterns, identify areas of excess or unnecessary spending, and take corrective actions to stay within budget.

- **It also serves as a basis for evaluating the business' financial performance.** Businesses can assess their efficiency, identify areas for improvement, and make informed decisions by comparing actual results to budgeted amounts.

Capital Budget

A capital budget is a financial plan that focuses on a company's long-term investments and expenditures. It entails budgeting for large projects and assets with long-term implications for the company's operations, expansion, and growth. The capital budget assists businesses in allocating funds for the acquisition, upgrade, or maintenance of fixed assets.

The capital budget serves several purposes for a business:

- **It assists businesses in planning and prioritizing large investments over time.** The capital budget considers the company's strategic goals and long-term growth plans, ensuring that funds are allocated to projects that promote long-term growth and competitiveness.

- **This budget ensures that the company's fixed assets are maintained and upgraded on time.** It helps to prevent asset deterioration, reduces operational disruptions, and ensures that the company has the necessary equipment and infrastructure to effectively support its operations.

  Furthermore, it assists businesses in controlling and monitoring their spending by allocating funds for capital expenditures in advance. It provides a framework for assessing the financial feasibility and profitability of capital projects, ensuring that investments are consistent with the company's financial resources and objectives.

- **The capital budget evaluates and manages the risks of long-term investments.** Businesses can make informed decisions, implement risk mitigation strategies, and reduce potential financial and operational risks by conducting a thorough analysis and evaluation.

- **This budget helps businesses determine the best financing options for capital projects.** It aids in determining the best mix of internal funds, debt financing, and external investments by taking into account factors such as cash flow, cost of capital, and the company's risk tolerance.

- **It also serves as the foundation for assessing the financial performance of capital investments.** Businesses can assess the effectiveness of their capital allocation decisions and make adjustments as needed by comparing actual results to budgeted amounts and tracking the returns generated by assets.

Cash Budget

A cash budget is a financial plan that outlines a company's projected cash inflows and outflows over a specific time period, usually monthly or quarterly. It focuses on managing and monitoring the business' cash flow in order to ensure adequate liquidity and meet financial obligations. The cash budget assists businesses in forecasting and controlling their cash position, allowing them to make informed spending, investment, and financing decisions.

The benefits of a cash budget for businesses include:

- **The cash budget allows businesses to track their cash flow.** It also ensures that they have enough money to meet their immediate financial obligations, such as payroll, rent, and supplier payments.

- **Businesses can effectively plan their financial activities by projecting cash inflows and outflows.** Based on their cash availability and requirements, they can make informed decisions about spending, investing, and financing.

- **The cash budget assists businesses in anticipating potential cash flow issues or shortfalls.** Recognizing and addressing these risks allows them to take appropriate steps to avoid financial difficulties or seek additional financing when necessary.

- **The cash budget provides valuable insight into a company's cash position.** It enables them to assess project financial viability, assess the impact of changes in expenses or revenue, and make informed decisions about resource allocation and investment opportunities.

- **It also serves as a reference point for tracking actual cash inflows and outflows.** A company's liquidity can be managed continuously by comparing actual performance to the budget on a regular basis.

Sales Budget

A sales budget is a financial plan that outlines a company's expected sales revenue over a specific time period. It is significant because it provides a clear projection of a company's expected sales performance. The sales budget assists businesses in setting realistic sales targets, allocating resources, and tracking progress toward revenue goals.

A sales budget has the following advantages:

- **The sales budget assists businesses in establishing specific sales targets and revenue goals.** It serves as a reference point against which actual sales performance can be measured and evaluated.

- **The sales budget helps businesses allocate resources more effectively by estimating sales volumes and revenue.** It helps determine production levels, inventory needs, staffing requirements, and marketing budgets to support the projected sales volume.

- **This budget also serves as a foundation for assessing actual sales performance.** Businesses can assess the effectiveness of their sales strategies, identify areas for improvement, and take corrective action if necessary by comparing budgeted sales revenue to actual sales revenue.

- **It also provides useful information for making informed decisions.** It assists businesses in determining the financial impact of various pricing strategies, product launches, market expansions, and changes in sales approaches.

- **The sales budget sets clear targets for the sales team.** This can drive motivation and performance.

Expense Budget

A monthly, quarterly, or annual expense budget is a financial plan that outlines the expected expenses and costs that a business will incur over a specific period. It provides a detailed breakdown of the various expenses required to run the business and aids in cost control, resource allocation, and financial performance monitoring.

The following are some of the advantages of a business expense budget:

- **The expense budget assists businesses in controlling costs and avoiding overspending.** Businesses can effectively track and manage their expenses by establishing specific budget limits for different expense categories.

- **It gives a clear picture of the expected expenses and helps businesses make informed decisions about resource allocation.** These resource allocations include staffing levels, inventory purchases, and operational investments.

- **It also serves as a standard for assessing the company's financial performance.** Businesses can assess their efficiency, identify areas for improvement, and take corrective action if necessary by comparing actual expenses to budgeted amounts.

- **The expense budget provides information that can be used to make informed decisions.** These decisions include cost-cutting initiatives, investments, or strategic changes.

Master Budget

The master budget is a comprehensive financial plan that combines all of a company's individual budgets and financial projections into a single, cohesive document. It gives an overview of the company's overall financial goals, objectives, and expectations for a specific time period, usually a year. The master budget acts as a business roadmap, guiding decision-making, resource allocation, and performance evaluation.

A master budget has the following advantages for a business:

- **By combining all relevant financial information into a single document, the master budget facilitates effective financial planning.** It gives a complete picture of the company's financial goals, expectations, and projections, guiding decision-making and resource allocation.

- **It assists businesses in setting specific financial goals and targets.** It establishes benchmarks for measuring performance and progress toward objectives.

- **This budget assists businesses in allocating funds.** These funds can go toward manpower, inventory, and other resources to support projected sales and operational needs.

- **Businesses can identify areas of strength, weakness, and opportunity for improvement.** This can be done by comparing actual results to budgeted amounts.

- **It also serves as a foundation for making sound financial decisions.** It assists businesses in assessing the financial impact of various scenarios, determining the viability of investments or expansion plans, and making data-driven decisions to optimize financial performance.

Budgeting Approaches

There are several approaches to budgeting, each with its own advantages and disadvantages. The choice of approach depends on an organization's size, complexity, industry, and management style. Some of the most common budgeting approaches include:

Incremental Budgeting

This approach involves using the previous year's budget as a starting point and making adjustments for the upcoming budget period. Changes are usually based on factors such as inflation, expected growth, or specific organizational goals. Incremental budgeting is relatively simple and easy to implement, but it may not encourage innovation or cost efficiency since it relies heavily on historical data.

Zero-Based Budgeting (ZBB)

In zero-based budgeting, every expense must be justified for each budget period, starting from a "zero base." This approach requires a thorough review of all activities and expenses, promoting cost efficiency and resource optimization. However, it can be time-consuming and may require significant effort from managers to justify their budget requests.

Activity-Based Budgeting (ABB)

Activity-based budgeting focuses on the costs of individual activities within an organization. This approach involves identifying the activities that drive costs, determining the resources required for each activity, and allocating budgets accordingly. ABB encourages cost control and process improvement by linking expenses to specific activities, but it can be complex and may require specialized software or expertise.

Rolling or Continuous Budgeting

Rolling budgets involve regularly updating the budget throughout the year, typically on a monthly or quarterly basis. As each period ends, a new period is added to the budget, ensuring that the organization always has a budget in place for the next 12 months. This approach allows for more accurate and timely financial planning, as well as greater flexibility in responding to changing business conditions. However, it can be more labor-intensive than other methods.

Top-Down Budgeting

In top-down budgeting, senior management sets the overall budget and then allocates resources to departments or divisions. This approach ensures that the budget aligns with strategic goals and priorities, but it may not consider the specific needs and challenges faced by individual departments.

Bottom-Up Budgeting

Bottom-up budgeting involves department managers creating their budgets based on their specific needs and objectives. These individual budgets are then consolidated into an overall organizational budget. This approach encourages greater involvement and accountability from department managers but can be time-consuming and may result in overly optimistic budget requests.

Each budgeting approach has its merits and drawbacks, and organizations should select the method that best aligns with their strategic goals, management style, and resource requirements. In some cases, a combination of approaches may be most effective for achieving a comprehensive and accurate budget.

Budgets clearly play an important role in business financial management. They provide a structured framework for financial planning, control, and evaluation. Businesses can set realistic goals, allocate resources efficiently, and track performance against targets by creating budgets. Businesses can use budgeting to make informed decisions, identify areas for improvement, and ensure financial stability and growth. A well-designed and effectively implemented budgeting process can improve financial discipline, optimize resource utilization, and contribute to an organization's overall success.

Forecasts

Businesses use forecasting to predict future outcomes and trends based on historical data, market conditions, and other relevant factors. It is an important part of strategic planning and decision-making because it allows businesses to anticipate and prepare for potential opportunities and challenges. Forecasts can cover a variety of business aspects, such as sales, revenue, expenses, cash flow, market demand, and industry trends. Businesses can forecast future periods, such as months, quarters, or years, by analyzing past performance, market research, and industry insights.

Gathering and analyzing data, identifying patterns and trends, and making predictions using statistical techniques or qualitative judgment are all parts of forecasting. Time series analysis, regression analysis, market research surveys, and expert opinions are among the forecasting methods available to businesses. Forecasting accurately provides businesses with valuable insights into how to allocate resources, plan for production, inventory management, pricing strategies, market campaigns, and overall company plans. It helps businesses align their actions with expected future conditions, mitigate risks, identify growth opportunities, and optimize their performance.

While forecasting can provide useful information, it is important to remember that it is not an exact science with many unknowns. Economic conditions, what competitors are doing, and market dynamics can all have an impact on forecast accuracy. Forecasts must be monitored, updated, and revised on a regular basis based on actual performance and results to be of real value.

Types of Forecasts

There are a number of types of forecasts businesses can use to plan for future outcomes and make informed decisions when planning for the future. These will depend on the type of business and its unique needs. Some of the common types of forecasts used include:

Sales Forecast

This forecast predicts future sales volume and revenue for a given time period. For example, a clothing retailer may forecast sales for the upcoming quarter using historical data, market trends, and seasonal patterns, allowing them to plan their inventory, marketing campaigns, and sales targets.

Financial Forecast

We examine future financial performance in this section, including revenues, expenses, profits, and cash flow. For example, a startup seeking funding may prepare a financial forecast for the next three years to show potential investors expected revenue growth, cost structure, and profitability.

Demand Forecast

In this section, we forecast future demand for a product or service. It assists businesses in determining production levels, inventory management, and resource allocation. A car manufacturer, for example, may forecast demand for specific vehicle models based on market trends, customer preferences, and economic indicators.

Budget Forecast

A budget forecast forecasts future financial activities and allocations based on the organization's budgeting process. It entails forecasting expenses, revenues, and cash flow in order to track performance against budgeted targets. For example, a department within a company may forecast its budget for the upcoming quarter, estimating costs for personnel, supplies, and other expenses.

Market Forecast

This forecast looks at the future trends, growth, and potential of a specific market or industry. It assists companies in evaluating market opportunities, competition, and customer behavior. For example, a technology company might analyze market forecasts for the smartphone industry to make decisions on future product development, marketing strategies, and market entry.

Staffing Forecast

This section forecasts a company's workforce requirements. It considers the number of employees, skills, and positions that are required. It helps with workforce planning, recruiting, and resource allocation. A retail chain may forecast staffing requirements during peak seasons using historical sales data and foot traffic patterns and plan employee schedules accordingly.

Forecasting Techniques

A company can forecast its future performance using a variety of techniques. These techniques may differ in scope and accuracy, as well as cost, and will be chosen based on the specific needs of the business. Qualitative techniques, time series analysis, and causal models are the three fundamental techniques employed.

Qualitative Techniques

These techniques rely on personal assessments, opinions, and insights from experts or individuals with knowledge and experience in the relevant field. When historical data is insufficient or untrustworthy, qualitative techniques are frequently used. Some of the common techniques used include:

- **Expert opinions:** Here, information is gathered from industry experts or professionals with extensive knowledge and experience in the field. A fashion retailer, for example, may consult with fashion designers, trend forecasters, and influencers to gain insight into upcoming fashion trends and make informed decisions about inventory and product offerings.

- **The Delphi method:** This technique is a structured approach that involves anonymously obtaining forecasts from a panel of experts. Individual forecasts from experts are then consolidated, and the process is repeated until a consensus is reached. This technique is useful when there are multiple points of view and the need to reduce biases. It can be used in a variety of fields, including technology, healthcare, and market research.

- **Market research:** Conducting surveys, focus groups, or interviews with customers, potential customers, or target market segments can provide valuable insights for forecasting. A food company, for example, may conduct market research to better understand consumer preferences, tastes, and purchasing habits in order to forecast demand for new product launches or variations of existing products.

- **Scenario analysis:** Entails creating and analyzing multiple scenarios based on various assumptions and potential future events. It assists businesses in anticipating the effects of various situations and developing contingency plans. For example, an energy company may use scenario analysis to forecast energy demand and pricing under various international or environmental conditions.

- **Historical comparisons:** This technique involves gaining insights from similar historical events or situations to the current situation. Businesses can make informed predictions about future outcomes by identifying comparable past events. For example, a tourism agency may forecast the potential impact on travel bookings based on historical data on travel patterns during economic downturns or global crises and adjust their marketing and pricing strategies accordingly.

It's crucial to keep in mind that qualitative techniques are subjective and subject to biases or limitations. They work best when combined with quantitative techniques and other data sources to improve forecast accuracy and reliability.

Time Series Analysis

This is a quantitative forecasting technique that entails analyzing historical data to identify patterns, trends, and seasonality in order to predict the future. It is especially useful when there is a large amount of historical data available. The technicalities of performing trend analysis are beyond the scope of this book's subject, and in most cases, specialized software systems are used to perform such in-depth analysis.

Here's an overview of time series analysis and an example:

- **Data collection:** Historical information is collected at regular intervals over a period of time. This data can be obtained from various sources, like sales records, financial statements, website traffic, or customer surveys.

- **Data investigation:** The data is examined to identify any underlying patterns or trends. This can be done visually, such as by plotting the data on a line graph, or statistically, by detecting patterns.

- **Data breakdown:** Data is broken down into its components, which typically include the trend, seasonality, and irregular or random changes. This helps in understanding the underlying trends and isolating them for forecasting purposes.

- **Modeling:** To develop a forecasting model, various statistical techniques such as moving averages, exponential smoothing, and ARIMA (autoregressive integrated moving average) models are applied to time series data. These models consider the data's identified patterns and relationships.

- **Forecasting:** Once the model is developed, it can be used to make future predictions by projecting the patterns and trends noticed in the historical data. The forecasted information can provide insights into future demand, sales, or other business indicators.

Example 9.1:

Suppose a retail store wants to forecast its monthly sales for the upcoming year. It collects historical sales data for the past five years, including the total sales figures for each month. By analyzing the time series data, the store identifies a clear seasonal pattern where sales are higher during the holiday season and lower during other months. Using time series analysis techniques such as seasonal breakdown and exponential contouring, the store develops a forecasting model. This model can then be used to predict the sales for each month in the upcoming year, taking into account the historical patterns and trends discovered in the data.

Time series analysis provides valuable insights into future patterns and trends, allowing businesses to make informed decisions about production, inventory management, resource allocation, and other issues.

Causal Method

This method for forecasting, also known as regression analysis, is a quantitative technique that establishes a relationship between the variable being forecasted and other independent variables that are believed to influence it. This method assumes that there is a cause-and-effect relationship between the variables. Here is an overview of the causal method and an example:

- **Determine variables:** The first step is to identify the variable to be forecasted (the dependent variable) as well as the independent variables that may be related to it. Economic indicators, demographic data, marketing campaigns, and any other relevant variables could be considered independent variables.

- **Data collection:** For both the dependent and independent variables, historical data is gathered. The data should be collected over a long enough period to capture the relationship between the variables.

- **Data analysis:** To examine the relationship between the dependent and independent variables, statistical techniques such as regression evaluation are used. The analysis aids in determining the relationship's strength and significance.

- **Model construction:** Based on the analysis, a mathematical model that quantifies the relationship between the variables is created. This model can then be used to forecast the dependent variable based on the values of the independent variables.

- **Forecasting:** Once the model has been developed, it can be used to predict the future values of the dependent variable by inputting the values of the independent variables. Forecasted values show how changes in the independent variables will affect the dependent variable.

Example 9.2:

Consider a manufacturing firm that wants to predict its monthly sales volume. It collects historical sales volume data (dependent variable) as well as data on factors that may influence sales, such as advertising expenditure, competitor pricing, and consumer confidence index (independent variables). The company establishes a relationship between sales volume and these independent variables by analyzing the data with regression analysis. Based on the values of the independent variables, the resulting regression model can be used to forecast sales volume for future periods.

When there is a known relationship between the dependent and independent variables, the causal method is useful for forecasting. It enables businesses to evaluate the impact of various factors on the variable being forecasted and make informed decisions based on those findings.

Quiz

1. What type of budget focuses on the allocation of financial resources for long-term investments such as equipment purchases or facility expansions?

   (A) Operating budget

   (B) Capital budget

   (C) Cash budget

   (D) Sales budget

2. Which type of cost remains constant regardless of the level of production or sales volume?

   (A) Fixed costs

   (B) Variable costs

   (C) One-time expenses

   (D) Cash flow

3. What type of budget is specifically designed to track and manage the cash inflows and outflows of a business?

   (A) Operating budget

   (B) Capital budget

   (C) Cash budget

   (D) Expense budget

4. Which budgeting technique involves estimating future financial performance based on historical data and trends?

    (A) Zero-based budgeting

    (B) Incremental budgeting

    (C) Rolling budgeting

    (D) Forecasting

5. Which type of forecasting method relies on expert opinions, market research, and subjective judgments to predict future business outcomes?

    (A) Time series analysis

    (B) Qualitative techniques

    (C) Causal method

    (D) None of the above

6. What type of forecasting focuses on historical data patterns to predict future trends and patterns?

    (A) Time series analysis

    (B) Qualitative techniques

    (C) Causal method

    (D) Regression analysis

7. Which forecasting method attempts to identify the cause-and-effect relationship between different variables to make predictions?

    (A) Time series analysis

(B) Qualitative techniques

(C) Causal method

(D) Regression analysis

8. **What forecasting technique involves analyzing the historical sales data of a product and using it to predict future sales?**

(A) Delphi method

(B) Market research

(C) Moving average

(D) None of the above

9. **Which forecasting method is best suited when there is limited historical data available, and subjective judgments and opinions are relied upon?**

(A) Delphi method

(B) Market research

(C) Historical analysis

(D) Expert opinions

For the answers to this and the other quizzes, visit MoneyMasterHQ.com/Books.

Chapter Takeaway

Finally, regardless of financial expertise, understanding the concepts of budgets and forecasts is critical for any business owner or manager. These practices lay the groundwork for making informed decisions, setting realistic goals, and achieving long-term success.

Forecasts help businesses anticipate market trends, demand fluctuations, and competitive forces by providing insights into future performance and potential opportunities or risks. With accurate forecasts, you can make proactive decisions, align resources, and adapt strategies to stay ahead of the competition in a rapidly changing business landscape.

These tools are not only for financial professionals. Budgets, forecasts, and business planning are practical and accessible tools that enable business owners and managers at all levels to make informed and strategic decisions. You can improve your company's performance, reduce risks, and seize new opportunities for growth and success by implementing these practices.

Segue to Next Chapter

In the following chapter, we will take a look at the world of management accounting, where financial data meets practical decision-making. Understanding the fundamentals of management accounting as a non-financial manager and/or business owner is critical for effectively managing your business, making informed decisions, and contributing to the overall success of your organization.

Chapter 10:

Management Accounting

Introduction to Management Accounting

Management accounting is the process of generating, analyzing, and interpreting financial information for internal decision-making purposes. It plays a crucial role in planning, controlling, and evaluating business operations. Management accounting focuses on providing timely and relevant information to managers, enabling them to make informed decisions about resource allocation, cost management, and performance evaluation. It encompasses various techniques and tools such as budgeting, costing systems, variance analysis, and key performance indicators.

As a non-financial manager, it is important to understand management accounting because it gives managers the information they need to make good financial decisions. It helps you figure out what the financial effects of different choices are, what the risks are, and what the most cost-effective course of action is. It also helps with planning and budgeting because it helps you set realistic financial goals, use your resources well, and keep track of how your business or department is doing compared to the goals you set. Also, it gives you a reliable way to measure how well your business or department is doing financially. So, managers can look at the income, expenses, and profits, find places to improve, and make changes as needed. In this way, managers can identify cost drivers, analyze cost behavior, and find ways to implement cost-saving measures to make their business more efficient and profitable.

Cost Concepts and Classification

Costs are an essential aspect of management accounting, as they impact pricing, profitability, and decision-making. Understanding different types of costs and their classification is crucial for effective cost management:

- **Direct costs:** These can be traced directly to a specific product (e.g., raw materials and direct labor). They are essential for determining product costs and making pricing decisions.

- **Indirect costs:** These cannot be attributed to a single product (e.g., rent, utilities, or salaries of support staff). They must be allocated to products or departments using an appropriate allocation method.

- **Fixed costs:** These remain constant regardless of production levels (e.g., rent, insurance, or depreciation). For an organization to be profitable, its revenues must cover its expenses.

- **Variable costs:** These change in proportion to production volume (e.g., raw materials, direct labor, or packaging). Understanding variable costs helps organizations manage production efficiency and break-even points.

- **Mixed costs:** These contain both fixed and variable components (e.g., electricity or sales commissions). Separating these components is crucial for accurate cost analysis and decision-making.

Costing Systems

Different costing systems are used to allocate costs to products or services based on an organization's needs, industry, and complexity:

- **Job order costing:** Suitable for custom or unique products, job order costing assigns costs to individual jobs or projects based on actual inputs (e.g., materials, labor, or overhead). This method provides accurate costing for specific jobs, which is useful for pricing and profitability analysis.

- **Process costing:** Used for mass-produced items, process costing distributes costs evenly across all units produced during a specific period. This approach simplifies the allocation of costs in industries with continuous production processes, such as manufacturing or chemical processing.

- **Activity-based costing (ABC):** This method allocates overhead costs to products or services based on the activities that drive those costs, providing more accurate cost information. ABC helps identify cost drivers and improve cost management by focusing on activities and their related costs.

Variance Analysis

Here, budgeted, or standard, costs are compared to actual results, and any differences are explained. It helps managers figure out how well different departments or activities are doing, find problems, and take steps to fix them. Variance analysis is often used to study and control costs like materials, labor, and overhead.

Budgeting and Forecasting

Budgets and forecasts are essential components of financial planning and control:

Budgets are financial plans that outline expected revenues, expenses, and cash flows for a specific period. They help organizations prioritize spending, manage cash flow, and monitor financial performance. Different types of budgets include master, operating, financial, and capital budgets, with various approaches such as incremental, zero-based, and rolling budgets.

Forecasting is the process of estimating future financial outcomes based on historical data, market research, and business trends. Forecasting helps organizations anticipate changes in the business environment, identify opportunities and risks, and make informed decisions. Forecasts can cover both short and long-term periods and are typically updated more frequently than budgets.

For a more detailed discussion on budgets and forecasts, please see Chapter 9.

Activity-Based Costing (ABC)

ABC is a cost-allocation method that assigns costs to specific activities or cost drivers. It gives a more precise picture of how costs are incurred in various processes or products. ABC assists managers in identifying the activities that have the greatest impact on costs and profitability, allowing them to make informed decisions about resource allocation, process improvement, and pricing strategies.

Let's use an example involving activity-based costing (ABC) to explain management accounting to a decision maker.

Scenario:

Suppose you manage a company that produces two types of widgets: Widget X and Widget Y. The non-finance manager needs to understand the cost allocation for each product, particularly overhead costs, to make informed decisions about pricing and resource allocation. The management accountant of the company provides you with the following information:

Production Costs:

Cost Category	Total Costs
Direct materials	$100,000
Direct labor	$80,000
Overhead	$120,000

Production Volume:

Product	Units Produced
Widget X	20,000
Wiget Y	10,000

Overhead Activities:

Activity	Cost Driver	Total Cost Driver Units
Machine setup	Number of setups	200
Quality control	Inspection hours	1,000
Packaging	Number of packages	30,000

Activity Rates:

Activity	Cost per Cost Driver Unit
Machine setup	$200
Quality control	$40
Packaging	$2

Step 1: Assign overhead costs to products using activity rates

First, calculate the overhead costs for each product based on the cost driver units consumed by each product:

Widget X:

Machine Setup: 150 setups * $200 = $30,000

Quality Control: 600 inspection hours * $40 = $24,000

Packaging: 20,000 packages * $2 = $40,000

Total Overhead: $30,000 + $24,000 + $40,000 = $94,000

Widget Y:

Machine Setup: 50 setups * $200 = $10,000

Quality Control: 400 inspection hours * $40 = $16,000

Packaging: 10,000 packages * $2 = $20,000

Total Overhead: $10,000 + $16,000 + $20,000 = $46,000

Step 2: Calculate total costs for each product

Add direct materials, direct labor, and overhead costs to find the total cost for each product:

Widget X:

Direct Materials: $60,000

Direct Labor: $48,000

Overhead: $94,000

Total Cost: $60,000 + $48,000 + $94,000 = $202,000

Widget Y:

Direct Materials: $40,000

Direct Labor: $32,000

Overhead: $46,000

Total Cost: $40,000 + $32,000 + $46,000 = $118,000

By providing a decision maker with this information, they can better understand the overhead allocation for each product using activity-based costing. This will help them make informed decisions about pricing, resource allocation, and cost management, ultimately improving the financial performance of the company. The ABC method provides a more accurate cost allocation compared to traditional methods, ensuring that the costs are distributed based on the actual consumption of resources by each product.

Relevant Costing

Relevant costing is a decision-making tool used in management accounting to help managers identify costs that are directly related to a specific decision. It focuses on analyzing the costs that will change or be affected by the decision while ignoring those that will remain unchanged. This approach helps managers make better-informed decisions by considering only the information that is pertinent to the situation at hand.

To explain relevant costs, let's use a simple example:

Imagine you manage a company that produces electronic devices, and one of the key components is a custom battery. You need to decide whether to continue manufacturing the batteries internally or outsource production to an external supplier.

To make this decision, you need to compare the costs associated with each option. However, not all costs should be considered. For example, your company's rent expense is not relevant to this decision, as it will remain the same regardless of whether you produce the batteries internally or outsource them.

Instead, you should focus on the costs that will change as a result of your decision. These may include:

- Direct material and labor costs for producing the batteries internally
- Variable overhead costs associated with internal production
- The purchase price per unit if you choose to outsource production

By focusing on these relevant costs, you can make a more informed decision about whether to continue producing batteries internally or outsource production to an external supplier.

In summary, relevant costing is a valuable tool that helps managers and business owners concentrate on the costs directly associated with a specific decision. By identifying and analyzing only the relevant costs, managers can make more effective decisions that contribute to the overall financial performance of the company.

Standard Costing and Variance Analysis

Standard costing and variance analysis are essential for cost control and performance evaluation:

- **Standard costing:** This method assigns predetermined costs to products or services, enabling comparison with actual costs. Standard costs are based on historical data, industry benchmarks, or engineering studies, providing a basis for performance evaluation and cost management.

- **Variance analysis:** This is the process of identifying and explaining the differences between standard and actual costs. Variance analysis focuses on direct materials, direct labor, and overhead variances. It helps organizations identify areas of inefficiency, implement corrective actions, and improve cost management.

Decision-Making and Relevant Costs

Effective decision-making requires considering relevant costs, which are those that will be affected by a specific decision:

- **Make or buy decisions:** Organizations must decide whether to produce goods internally or outsource production to external suppliers. Relevant costs in this decision include production costs, outsourcing costs, and opportunity costs.

- **Special order decisions:** When an organization receives a non-recurring order at a different price or volume, it must assess the impact on revenues, variable costs, and capacity constraints, considering relevant costs and benefits.

- **Product mix decisions:** Organizations must determine the optimal mix of products or services to maximize profitability, taking relevant costs, market demand, and production constraints into account.

Performance Evaluation and Management Control

Performance evaluation and management control involve assessing the effectiveness and efficiency of an organization's operations:

- **Key Performance Indicators (KPIs):** Quantitative or qualitative measures that reflect an organization's performance in achieving its objectives, KPIs help managers monitor progress and identify areas for improvement.

- **Balanced Scorecard:** A strategic performance management tool that incorporates financial and non-financial measures, the balanced scorecard provides a comprehensive view of an organization's performance and ensures alignment with strategic goals.

- **Responsibility accounting:** This approach assigns responsibility for financial performance to specific departments or managers, promoting accountability and enabling more accurate performance evaluation.

Financial Statement Analysis for Management Accounting

Financial statement analysis is essential for understanding an organization's financial position and performance:

- **Ratio analysis:** Ratios provide insights into liquidity, solvency, profitability, and efficiency, helping managers evaluate performance and identify trends.

- **Trend analysis:** Examining changes in financial data over time, trend analysis helps organizations assess performance, anticipate future developments, and make strategic decisions.

- **Common-size analysis:** By expressing financial statement items as percentages of a common base, common-size analysis enables comparison across companies or industries, regardless of size.

Strategic Management Accounting

Strategic management accounting supports competitive advantage by integrating financial information with strategic planning:

- **Value chain analysis:** By assessing the activities involved in creating and delivering products or services, value chain analysis helps organizations identify opportunities to enhance value and reduce costs.

- **Target costing:** Focusing on the desired cost for a product to achieve a specific profit margin, target costing involves setting cost targets and aligning design, production, and marketing efforts to achieve those targets.

- **Customer profitability analysis**: Examining the revenues and costs associated with different customer segments, customer profitability analysis helps organizations prioritize customers and allocate resources effectively.

- **Strategic cost management:** Integrating cost management with strategic planning, this approach focuses on achieving sustainable competitive advantage through cost leadership, differentiation, or niche strategies.

Decision Analysis

Decision analysis means weighing various options and deciding on the best course of action based on financial and non-financial considerations. Techniques like cost-benefit analysis, incremental analysis, and capital budgeting help managers make decisions about investments, product mix, outsourcing pricing, and other issues.

Let's use an example involving make-or-buy analysis to explain management accounting.

Scenario:

Suppose you manage a company that produces electronic devices, and one of the key components is a custom circuit board. The manager needs to decide whether to continue manufacturing the circuit boards internally or outsource production to an external supplier.

As a management accountant, you provide them with the following cost information:

Internal Production Costs:

Cost Category	Amount per Circuit Board
Direct materials	$15
Direct labor	$10
Variable overhead	$5
Fixed overhead	$8
Total	$38

External Supplier Quote:

Cost Category	Amount per Circuit Board
Purchase price	$30

Annual Demand: 10,000 circuit boards

Step 1: Calculate the total cost under each option

Total Internal Production Cost = (Direct Materials + Direct Labor + Variable Overhead + Fixed Overhead) * Annual Demand

Total Internal Production Cost = ($15 + $10 + $5 + $8) * 10,000 = $380,000

Total External Purchase Cost = Purchase Price * Annual Demand

Total External Purchase Cost = $30 * 10,000 = $300,000

Step 2: Analyze the results

Comparing the total costs under each option, we can see that outsourcing production to the external supplier would result in a cost savings of $80,000 per year ($380,000 - $300,000).

By providing the manager with this information, they can better understand the cost implications of their make-or-buy decision. In this case, outsourcing the production of circuit boards would result in significant cost savings, so the manager might decide to choose this option. However, it's important to consider other factors, such as quality control, lead times, and supplier reliability, before making a final decision. Management accounting helps managers make informed decisions by providing accurate and relevant financial information that considers various aspects of the business.

Limitations of Management Accounting

Like any other approach, management accounting has certain limitations, and it is important to be aware of these. Some common limitations include:

- **Subjectivity:** Estimations and judgments in management accounting are based on personal opinions. Things like assumptions, forecasts, and allocation methods can add a subjective element to the analysis. If subjectivity is not taken into account carefully, it can sometimes lead to biased or wrong results.

- **Data limitations:** The quality of the data used determines how accurate and reliable management accounting information is. Data that is wrong or incomplete can lead to wrong analysis and decisions. Gathering and keeping relevant and reliable data can be hard, especially in large organizations with complicated operations.

- **Time and cost limitations:** Comprehensive management accounting analyses may take a long time and be expensive. Organizations with limited resources may not have the time or money to do a lot of analysis. Because of this, management accounting may not be able to give full insights and may instead use simplified models and assumptions.

- **Financial variables and focus:** Management accounting gives valuable financial information, but it may not take into account all relevant non-financial factors. Financial data may not show how important things like customer satisfaction, employee morale, and the impact on the environment are. For well-rounded decisions, managers should think about both financial and non-financial factors.

- **Inaccuracy in forecasting:** Management accounting relies on historical data and assumptions to make projections and forecasts, which means that they are not always accurate. But the future is unknown, and unplanned events can have a big effect on what actually happens. Forecasts and projections should not be taken as exact predictions, but rather as estimates.

- **Overly focused on immediate outcomes:** Management accounting often focuses on short-term performance measures, such as quarterly or yearly results. Focusing on short-term goals can sometimes make people forget about long-term strategies. It is important for managers to find a balance between short-term financial goals and long-term goals for growth and sustainability.

Even with these problems, management accounting is still a very useful branch of accounting for analyzing information, making decisions, and judging performance. By understanding the limits of management accounting and using it in conjunction with other sources of information, managers can improve how they make decisions and drive the success of their organizations.

Quiz

1. Which of the following is the primary goal of management accounting?

(A) Preparing financial statements for external users

(B) Providing information for internal decision-making

(C) Ensuring compliance with tax regulations

(D) Evaluating investment opportunities

2. What types of costs can be directly traced to a specific product or service?

(A) Direct costs

(B) Indirect costs

(C) Fixed costs

(D) Sunk costs

3. Which costing system assigns costs to individual jobs or projects based on actual inputs, making it suitable for custom or unique products?

(A) Job order costing

(B) Process costing

(C) Activity-based costing

(D) Standard costing

4. What is the main objective of variance analysis in management accounting?

(A) Identifying and explaining differences between standard and actual costs

(B) Calculating the break even point for each product

(C) Allocating overhead costs to products or services

(D) Evaluating the profitability of different customer segments

5. In activity-based costing, what is the term used for the activities that drive overhead costs?

(A) Cost drivers

(B) Cost pools

(C) Cost centers

(D) Cost objects

6. Which of the following decisions would require considering relevant costs in management accounting?

(A) Make or buy decisions

(B) Special order decisions

(C) Product mix decisions

(D) All of the above

7. Break-even analysis

Company ABC produces and sells a single product. The following information is available for the product:

- Selling price per unit: $25

- Variable cost per unit: $15

- Total fixed costs: $50,000

Calculate the break-even point in units and sales revenue.

8. **Company XYZ is considering whether to continue producing a component in-house or outsource it to an external supplier. The following information is available:**

- Internal production cost per unit: $12 (including $3 of allocated fixed overhead)

- External supplier quote per unit: $9

- Annual demand: 10,000 units

- The decision won't have an impact on the fixed overhead costs allocated.

9. **Should Company XYZ produce the component in-house or outsource it?** Calculate the total relevant costs for each alternative.

For the answers to this and the other quizzes, visit
MoneyMasterHQ.com/Books.

Chapter Takeaway

In this chapter on management accounting, we delved into various important topics that are fundamental for effective decision-making and performance evaluation within an organization. We explored cost concepts and their classification, different costing systems, cost-volume-profit analysis, variance analysis, budgeting and forecasting, activity-based costing, relevant costing, standard costing, and variances, decision making with relevant costing, performance evaluation and management control, financial statement analysis, strategic management accounting, and decision analysis.

Cost concepts and classification are crucial for accurately measuring and analyzing costs incurred by the organization. Understanding different costing systems, enables the allocation of costs and products or services based on their unique characteristics and production processes. Cost-volume-profit analysis helps in understanding the relationship between costs, volume, and profitability, guiding decisions regarding pricing, sales volume, and cost optimization.

Variance analysis compares actual results with planned or expected results, identifying areas for improvement and enabling cost control and corrective actions. Budgeting and forecasting involve setting financial targets, estimating future revenues and expenses, and allocating resources effectively for planning, controlling, and evaluating performance.

Activity-Based Costing (ABC) focuses on identifying and allocating costs based on activities performed, providing a more accurate understanding of product and service costs. Relevant costing considers only the costs and revenues relevant to a specific decision, aiding decision making regarding pricing, product discontinuation, outsourcing, and special orders.

Standard costing establishes predetermined costs for materials, labor, and overheads, with variances calculated to identify inefficiencies and support corrective actions. Performance evaluation and management control involve comparing actual results with predetermined goals and benchmarks, aligning objectives, and providing feedback.

Financial statement analysis helps assess the financial health and performance of the organization by analyzing ratios, trends, and indicators. Strategic management accounting incorporates market trends, competitive intelligence, and non-financial factors to support strategic planning and implementation.

Finally, decision analysis employs quantitative techniques, such as cost-benefit analysis and risk assessment, to evaluate alternative courses of action and make optimal decisions in uncertain situations.

Financial excellence is not a destination but an ongoing journey of continuous improvement. Peter Drucker, the father of modern management, said: "You can't manage what you can't measure." By consistently implementing these strategies and insights, non-finance managers and business owners can not only elevate their company's financial performance but also empower themselves to make informed decisions that drive the overall success of their organization. In the pursuit of excellence, knowledge and measurement become the keys to unlocking your business' true potential.

Segue to Next Chapter

The concept of the break-even point is critical in financial analysis and decision making. As a non-financial manager, you must understand this concept in order to effectively assess the financial health and viability of business operations. In the following chapter, we will deconstruct the break-even point by providing a step-by-step explanation of its calculation and interpretation. We will look at the various components that go into a break-even analysis, such as fixed costs, variable costs, and pricing strategies.

Chapter 11:

The Importance of Break-Even

and Why It Matters

Business is a balancing act, with cost and revenue as the two key players on the seesaw. The break-even point? It's the fulcrum where the seesaw is perfectly balanced. –Anonymous

What Is Meant by the Break-Even Point?

In this chapter, we delve into a fundamental financial concept that every non-finance manager should be familiar with: break-even analysis.

Picture yourself on a hike. Wouldn't you want to know the distance to your destination? Similarly, in business, it's beneficial to understand how much you need to sell to cover all your costs and start generating profits. This equilibrium point is what we refer to as the "break-even point."

But before we plunge into the depths of break-even analysis, let's start by dipping our toes into some foundational concepts.

The break-even point is the point at which the company's total income equals its total expenses. In other words, it is when the company makes just as much money as it is spending, and there is no profit or loss.

To understand the break-even point, we need to first look at fixed costs and variable costs:

- **Fixed costs are expenses that remain constant regardless of the level of production or sales.** They include costs like rent, salaries, utilities, and insurance. These costs do not change in the short term, regardless of whether the company is selling a few products or a large volume.

- **Variable costs can fluctuate based on the level of production or sales.** They include costs like raw materials, direct labor, and sales, and these costs increase as the company produces or sells more products or services.

How Is the Break-Even Point Calculated?

The break-even point is calculated by dividing the fixed costs by the difference between the selling price per unit and variable cost per unit. The resulting figure represents the number of units the company needs to sell to cover all its costs.

Example 11.1:

ABC Furniture sells wooden chairs. The company has fixed costs of $10,000 per month, and each chair has a variable cost of $20. The selling price per chair is $50.

To calculate the break-even point:

Break-even point

= fixed costs / (selling price per unit - variable cost per unit)

= $10,000 / ($50 - $20)

= $10,000 / $30

= 333.33 chairs.

Let's now calculate the profit or loss at this point to prove that this is actually the break-even point.

The Importance of the Break-Even Point

The main reasons why the break-even point is important for a business are:

- **Financial planning:** Knowing the break-even point helps with financial planning and decisions. It allows for realistic sales targets and determines how much of a product or service needs to be produced to cover costs. Without this information, budgeting, resource allocation, and setting pricing strategies are very difficult.

- **Profitability analysis:** The break-even point is used to determine profitability. It assists businesses in understanding the impact of changes in sales, volume, or pricing on their bottom line. Businesses can determine whether they are making a profit or losing money by comparing actual sales to the break-even point.

- **Controlling costs:** The break-even point emphasizes the importance of controlling costs. Businesses can analyze their fixed and variable costs to find ways to cut costs. They can then implement cost-cutting measures and improve their financial performance by understanding the cost structure and its impact on the break-even point.

- **Pricing decisions:** In order to set appropriate prices for products or services, the company must first determine the break-even point. A company can make realistic pricing decisions that keep profit margins, market demand, and cost structure in mind and allow them to reach the break-even point and achieve profitability.

- **Risk assessment:** By comparing the break-even point to actual and projected sales, businesses can assess their vulnerability to changes in market conditions, competition, and other external factors. This can assist a company in identifying current and potential risks and implementing risk-mitigation strategies.

- **Business viability:** If a company consistently falls short of the break-even point, it may need to reconsider its business strategy and take the necessary steps to rectify the situation and ensure profitability.

The break-even point is an important indicator of a company's financial success or failure, influencing cost structure, pricing strategies, and overall viability.

Cost-Volume-Profit (CVP) Analysis

Cost-Volume-Profit (CVP) analysis is a powerful tool for understanding the inter-relationships among costs, sales volume, and profit:

- **Break-even analysis:** This determines the sales level at which total revenues equal total costs, indicating the point where an organization neither makes a profit nor incurs a loss. Break-even analysis helps organizations set sales targets and assess the impact of changes in costs or prices.

- **Contribution margin:** The difference between sales revenue and variable costs, the contribution margin, which represents the amount available to cover fixed costs and generate profit. It provides insights into product profitability and helps evaluate the financial viability of different products or services.

- **Sensitivity analysis:** This technique assesses the impact of changes in variables (e.g., price, volume, or costs) on profit, helping organizations anticipate risks, identify opportunities, and make informed decisions.

Let's use an example involving break-even analysis and cost-volume-profit (CVP) analysis to explain management accounting.

Scenario:

Suppose you own a bakery that sells two types of cakes: chocolate and vanilla cake. It is important to understand the break-even point for each product and the impact of changes in production volume on profitability. The management accountant of the company provides you with the following information:

Product Costs and Selling Prices:

Product	Fixed Costs	Variable Costs per Unit	Selling Price per Unit
Chocolate cake	$10,000	$6	$12
Vanilla cake	$8,000	$4	$8

Step 1: Calculate the contribution margin per unit for each product

Contribution Margin per Unit = Selling Price per Unit - Variable Costs per Unit

Chocolate Cake: $12 - $6 = $6

Vanilla Cake: $8 - $4 = $4

Step 2: Calculate the break-even point for each product

Break-Even Point (Units) = Fixed Costs / Contribution Margin per Unit

Chocolate Cake: $10,000 / $6 = 1,667 units

Vanilla Cake: $8,000 / $4 = 2,000 units

Step 3: Analyze the results

The break-even analysis shows the number of units that must be sold for each product to cover its fixed and variable costs, resulting in zero profit. In this case, the bakery needs to sell 1,667 units of chocolate cake and 2,000 units of vanilla cake to break even.

Step 4: Perform a CVP analysis

Cost-Volume-Profit (CVP) analysis examines the relationship between costs, sales volume, and profit. Using the contribution margin per unit, we can explore the impact of changes in production volume on profitability.

For example, if the bakery increases the sales volume of chocolate cake by 500 units, the additional profit generated would be:

Additional Profit = Contribution Margin per Unit * Additional Units Sold

Additional Profit = $6 * 500 = $3,000

Conclusion:

By having the above kind of information, a decision maker can better understand the break-even point for each product and the impact of changes in production volume on profitability. This will help them make informed decisions about production levels, pricing strategies, and resource allocation, ultimately improving the financial performance of the bakery. The break-even point will be discussed in detail in the next chapter.

Quiz

1. The break-even point is the level of sales or activity at which:

(A) The company incurs a loss

(B) The company covers all its costs

(C) The company achieves maximum profitability

(D) The company shuts down operations

2. Fixed costs are expenses that:

(A) Fluctuate based on production or sales

(B) Remain constant regardless of production or sales

(C) Are incurred only during peak seasons

(D) Depend on the market demand

3. The break-even point can be calculated by:

(A) Dividing fixed costs by variable costs

(B) Dividing variable costs by fixed costs

(C) Dividing fixed costs by the contribution margin

(D) Dividing total revenue by total costs

4. The break-even point helps business in:

(A) Setting unrealistic sales targets

(B) Assessing profitability

(C) Evaluating risk associated with operations

(D) Avoiding the need for financial planning

5. If a company's actual sales exceed the break-even point, it means:

(A) The company is operating at a loss

(B) The company is incurring high variable costs

(C) The company is generating a profit

(D) The company is not covering its fixed costs

For the answers to this and the other quizzes, visit
MoneyMasterhq.com/Books.

Chapter Takeaway

In this chapter on the break-even point, we explored an important concept in financial management that is important for non-financial managers to grasp. The break-even point is the level of sales at which a business neither earns a profit nor incurs a loss. It is the critical threshold that helps managers assess the financial viability of their operations and make informed decisions. It provides valuable insights into the relationship between costs, sales volume, and profitability. By understanding and determining the break-even point, managers can understand the minimum level of sales necessary to cover costs and begin generating profits.

The break-even point serves as a benchmark for performance evaluation. Managers can set targets beyond the break-even point to achieve their goal. This provides a clear indication to sales personnel of what the minimum achievement should be to keep the organization profitable. Managers are able to use the break-even analysis to evaluate the financial implications of various decisions, like introducing new products, expanding operations, and changing pricing strategies. By understanding the break-even point, managers can assess the feasibility of proposed changes.

Segue to Next Chapter

In the next chapter, we will delve into the world of investment divisions and explore the intricacies of debt and equity. By understanding the principles and practices associated with these topics, we can gain insight into how businesses can strategically allocate resources, raise capital, and optimize their overall financial structure.

Chapter 12:

Investments, Debt, and Equity

Evaluating New Investments

When businesses evaluate new investments, they can find opportunities that could lead to higher returns. Companies can make the best use of their resources and get the most out of their investments by choosing which investment options are financially viable and likely to be profitable. Capital and people are two examples of limited resources that need to be carefully allocated. Evaluating investments helps businesses set priorities and put their resources toward projects that align with their strategic goals and have the best chance of success. This makes sure that resources are used in the best way possible.

There is always some risk when making an investment. By evaluating new investments, businesses can figure out and deal with the possible risks that come with projects. Companies can make good decisions and put plans in place to reduce risks if they do thorough risk assessments and consider factors like market conditions, competition, and changes to regulations.

By evaluating new investments, you can make sure they fit with the business' overall strategic direction. The investments should help the company reach its long-term goals, grow, and stay competitive. By thinking about strategic fit, businesses can focus on investments that build on their strengths and give them an edge over their competitors. The capital budgeting process includes evaluating new investments. It helps businesses make the best use of their capital resources by finding the projects that have the best chance of generating positive cash flows and creating long-term value. This makes sure that money is spent on projects that support the company's financial goals. Evaluating investments helps businesses make decisions that are good for their long-term success. By looking at things like market trends, new technologies, and changing customer tastes, businesses can find investment opportunities that can drive growth, innovation, and the ability to adapt to a constantly changing business landscape.

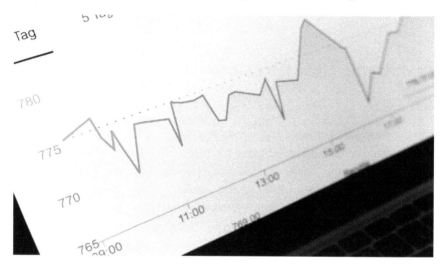

Methods to Evaluate New Investments

To effectively evaluate new investments, it is essential to consider both quantitative and qualitative factors. Quantitative factors include the projected financial returns, such as cash flows, net present value (NPV), internal rate of return (IRR), payback period, profitability index, ROI, and risk analysis. These metrics help managers assess the potential profitability of an investment and compare it to alternative options or a required rate of return.

In addition to the financial aspects, qualitative factors play a significant role in evaluating new investments. These may include the strategic fit with the company's vision and goals, competitive advantages, market demand, and potential risks associated with the investment. By considering both quantitative and qualitative factors, managers can gain a holistic understanding of an investment's potential impact on the organization.

As businesses navigate an ever-changing economic landscape, the ability to identify and capitalize on profitable investment opportunities is critical to maintaining a competitive edge. By developing a strong foundation for evaluating new investments, managers can drive informed decision-making, optimize resource allocation, and contribute to the organization's long-term success.

Note the examples that follow in the below sections: The actual methodology of calculating the below is beyond the scope of this book, but the below are a few examples of how this is generally done. Do not worry if you do not fully understand this area as it is more technical, but having a general idea of the names of these methods and how to arrive at the decision of what is a good project or not (e.g., a lower payback period being better, a higher net present value being better, and so on) would be sufficient.

Payback Period

This method figures out how long it will take for an investment to get back its initial cost. It looks at how long it takes for the money that comes in from the investment to equal the money that went out at the start. The better the investment, the shorter the time it takes for the money to come back.

Imagine your company is considering investing in a new machine that costs $100,000 and is expected to generate annual cash inflows of $25,000 for the next 6 years. The payback period calculates how long it takes for the investment to recover its initial cost.

Payback Period = Initial Investment / Annual Cash Inflow

Payback Period = $100,000 / $25,000 = 4 years

In this example, it will take 4 years for the company to recover the initial cost of the machine. If there was another machine that had a payback period of three years, it may be a better option, provided other factors are also taken into account.

Net Present Value (NPV)

NPV is a way to calculate how profitable an investment is by bringing the expected future cash flows from the investment into the present. As we mentioned previously, $1 in 10 years is not the same as $1 today primarily given the difference of what it can buy today versus in 10 years. Therefore, it is important to make cash flows of 10 years comparable to today's cash flow. This conversion is performed through the process of what is called discounting future cash flows to the present value.

It takes into account the change in value of money over time and gives a net value that shows the difference between the present value of cash coming in and going out. If the NPV is positive, it means that the investment could be profitable.

Let's use the same example as above, but now consider the time value of money (i.e., $1 today is not the same as $1 in 10 years, and what you can purchase from this $1 now versus in 10 years is very different).

Your company's required rate of return is 8%. NPV calculates the difference between the present value of cash inflows and the initial investment.

Year	Cash Flow	Discount Factor (8%)	Present Value
0	-$100,000	1,000	-$100,000
1	$25,000	0.926	$23,150
2	$25,000	0.857	$21,425
3	$25,000	0.794	$19,850
4	$25,000	0.735	$18,375
5	$25,000	0.681	$17,025
6	$25,000	0.630	$15,750

NPV = Sum of Present Values - Initial Investment

NPV = $111,575 - $100,000 = $11,575

A positive NPV indicates that the project is expected to generate more value than the required rate of return.

Internal Rate of Return (IRR)

IRR is the discount rate at which the NPV of an investment becomes zero. Using the same example, the IRR can be calculated using financial software or iterative methods. In this case, the IRR is approximately 12.2%. Since the IRR is higher than the required rate of return (8%), the project is considered a good investment.

Profitability Index (PI)

The PI is calculated by dividing the present value of cash inflows by the present value of cash outflows. It shows how much the investment will cost and how much money it is expected to bring in. If the PI is more than one, it means that the investment was profitable.

Return on Investment (ROI)

ROI measures the profitability of an investment as a percentage of the initial investment. Using the same example, assume the machine has a salvage value of $10,000 after 6 years.

Total Cash Inflows = ($25,000 * 6) + $10,000 = $160,000

Net Profit = Total Cash Inflows - Initial Investment = $160,000 - $100,000 = $60,000

ROI = (Net Profit / Initial Investment) * 100

ROI = ($60,000 / $100,000) * 100 = 60%

The ROI indicates that for every dollar invested, the company earns a return of 60 cents.

Risk Analysis

Risk analysis involves evaluating the uncertainties and potential challenges associated with an investment. For example, a company plans to launch a new product with projected sales of 5,000 units per year at a price of $50 per unit. However, there's a possibility that sales could be lower (3,000 units) or higher (7,000 units) due to market conditions.

A simple risk analysis might involve calculating the expected revenue under different sales scenarios:

Low Sales: 3,000 units * $50 = $150,000

Expected Sales: 5,000 units * $50 = $250,000

High Sales: 7,000 units * $50 = $350,000

By considering various scenarios, managers can better understand the potential risks and rewards associated with the investment.

Qualitative Factors

In addition to financial metrics, qualitative factors are also taken into account when judging an investment. These may include market trends, the outlook for the industry, a competitive analysis, new technologies, effects on the environment, and how well the investment fits with the strategic goals of the company.

Remember that there is no one way to judge an investment as a whole. Businesses often use more than one of these methods to get a full picture of an investment opportunity and make smart decisions. Methods will be chosen based on things like the type of investment, the standards of the industry, and the needs and preferences of the business.

Comparison of the Various Methods

Method	Measure of Success
Payback period	A shorter payback period is better
Net Present Value (NPV)	A higher NPV is better
Internal Rate of Return	A higher IRR (above required rate) is better
Return on investment (ROI)	A higher ROI is better
Profitability index	A higher profitability index is better
Risk analysis	A lower risk with a higher potential reward is better

Method	Pros	Cons
Payback period	Simple and easy to understand	Ignores time value of money
	Useful for liquidity analysis	Does not consider cash flows beyond payback period
Net Present Value (NPV)	Considers time value of money	Requires an accurate estimation of the discount rate
	Measures total value created	Can be complex to calculate
Internal Rate of Return (IRR)	Considers the time value of money	Assumes reinvestment at IRR which may not be realistic

Method	Pros	Cons
	Provides a single percentage for easy comparison	May produce multiple solutions in projects with unconventional cash flows
Return on investment (ROI)	Easy to understand	Ignores time value of money
	Allows comparison across different investments	Does not provide information about the investment's duration or scale
Profitability index	Considers time value of money	Requires an accurate estimation of the discount rate
	Allows comparison of projects with different sizes	May not be suitable for mutually exclusive projects
Risk analysis	Helps identify potential challenges and uncertainties	Difficult to quantify all risks
	Encourages scenario planning and contingency measures	Subjective and based on assumptions

Evaluation of new investments is a key part of business division. Using tools like the payback period net present value, internal rate of return, profitability index, return on investment, risk analysis, and qualitative factors, businesses can figure out if an investment opportunity is viable and could make money. Each method has its own pros and cons, which lets managers think about different parts of an investment. In the end, a thorough evaluation method that uses both quantitative and qualitative analysis helps businesses make smart investment decisions, maximize their returns, and keep risks under control.

Debt and Equity

Debt and equity are two primary ways companies can raise capital to fund their operations, grow, and invest in new projects. Understanding these concepts is essential for anyone learning about finance. Let's examine their characteristics and provide an example for each.

Debt

Debt refers to money that a business borrows from external sources and must repay over time, usually with interest. It is a form of financing that allows businesses to access funds for various purposes, such as expanding operations, purchasing assets, or managing cash flow.

Example 12.1:

Sweet Delights, a small bakery, wishes to increase its production capacity. They do not, however, have enough cash on hand to purchase new baking equipment. Sweet Delights approaches a bank and applies for a loan to fund its expansion. The bank approves the loan and lends them the funds they require. Sweet Delights incurs debt as a result of the loan amount. The bakery is now responsible for repaying the loan amount to the bank within a certain time frame, usually with a finance charge attached. They will make monthly or quarterly payments to gradually pay off the debt over time.

Sweet Delights incurs interest as an additional cost when borrowing money. It is a percentage of the loan that the bakery pays to the bank in exchange for the risk and opportunity cost of lending the funds. The terms of the loan agreement, the current interest rate, and the bakery's creditworthiness are typically the determining factors of the interest rate. Sweet Delights can expand its production capacity by incurring debt. However, the bakery must responsibly manage its debt and ensure that the business generates enough cash flow to make timely loan payments and cover interest expenses.

Debt enables businesses to obtain the funds they require to grow and operate. However, it is critical to carefully evaluate the debt's terms and conditions, plan for repayment, and consider the impact of interest expenses on the financial health of the business.

Equity

The ownership of a business is referred to as equity. When a company is starting out or needs more capital, it can raise funds by offering ownership shares to investors in exchange for their investment. These ownership stakes are referred to as equity or equity financing.

Example 12.2:

A tech startup called Tech Innovators needs funds to develop and launch a new software product. Instead of borrowing money or taking on debt, the company decides to seek equity financing. They approach potential investors and offer them the opportunity to become shareholders in the company by purchasing equity shares.

Investors who are interested in the potential success of Tech Innovators can choose to invest in the company by buying a certain number of shares. In return, they become part owners of the business and are entitled to a portion of its profits and assets. This ownership interest represents their equity stake in the company.

Unlike debt, equity does not need to be repaid with interest over a specific period. Instead, equity investors share in the company's financial success or failure. If Tech Innovators perform well and generate profits, the shareholders may receive dividends or see an increase in the value of shares. On the other hand, if the company faces losses, the shareholders may experience a decrease in the value of their investment.

Equity financing allows businesses like Tech Innovators to raise capital without incurring debt. It can provide long-term funding for business operations, expansion, research and development, and other strategic initiatives. Additionally, equity investors can bring valuable expertise, networks, and support to the business. But, by offering equity, business owners dilute their ownership and control over the company. They may need to consult with shareholders and consider their opinions when making important business decisions. Additionally, if the business becomes highly successful, the shareholders may expect a higher return on their investment, which could result in reduced profitability for the original owners.

Equity financing offers businesses the opportunity to raise funds and share ownership with investors. It can provide long-term support and resources for growth. But, business owners should carefully consider the trade-offs and implications of diluting their ownership.

Debt vs Equity

Advantages of Debt Financing:

- Debt interest payments are generally tax deductible, which can reduce the company's overall tax burden.

- When a company incurs debt, it does not dilute the ownership or control of its existing owners. They retain full ownership and decision-making authority.

- Debt has a predetermined repayment schedule, which allows businesses to plan their cash flow and budget accordingly.

- Debt payments are typically fixed, allowing businesses to better forecast and manage their expenses.

Disadvantages of Debt Financing:

- Businesses that incur debt are required by law to repay the principal amount plus interest, regardless of their financial performance. Failure to repay the debt can result in negative consequences, such as legal action or harm to the company's credit rating.

- Debt incurs interest costs, which add to the overall expenses of the business and can have an impact on profitability.

- If a company cannot generate enough cash flow to meet its debt obligations, it may face financial distress or even bankruptcy.

Advantages of Equity Financing:

- In contrast to debt, equity financing does not necessitate repayment of funds. Investors share in the company's success or failure and do not expect a fixed return on their investment.

- Equity investors and business owners are both sharing the risk. If the company fails, they absorb the losses, relieving the owners of the burden.

- Equity investors frequently bring valuable expertise, industry knowledge, and networks that can aid in the growth and development of a business.

- When compared to debt financing, equity financing allows businesses to raise larger amounts of capital, especially for high-growth ventures.

Disadvantages of Equity Financing:

- By issuing equity, business owners relinquish some of their ownership and control over the company. They may need to consult with shareholders and take their feedback into account during decision-making processes.

- Equity investors are entitled to a portion of the company's profits. This can reduce the original owner's overall profitability.

- Conflicts of interest can arise when there are many shareholders because different shareholders may have different goals and objectives for the business.

When deciding between debt and equity financing, businesses must carefully consider their specific circumstances, financial goals, and risk tolerance. Some businesses may benefit from a hybrid approach that strikes a balance between the benefits and drawbacks of each option.

The decision-makers of a company should pay close attention to the risks of a debt spiral. A debt spiral occurs when a company takes on additional debt to service existing debt obligations, resulting in an unsustainable cycle of increasing debt levels and interest payments.

This situation can lead to financial distress and, ultimately, bankruptcy if the company is unable to generate sufficient cash flow to meet its debt obligations. Thus, it's crucial for companies to carefully manage their debt levels and ensure they can comfortably service their debt to avoid falling into a debt spiral.

Take Lehman Brothers for example. The investment bank filed for bankruptcy in 2008 during the global financial crisis, primarily due to its excessive leverage and exposure to subprime mortgage-backed securities. Unable to meet its debt obligations, Lehman Brothers became the largest bankruptcy filing in U.S. history at that time.

Quiz

1. **Which financing option generally provides tax-deductible interest payments?**

   (A) Debt

   (B) Equity

2. Debt financing allows businesses to retain:

(A) Ownership and control

(B) Expertise and networks

3. Which financing option requires a predetermined repayment schedule?

(A) Debt

(B) Equity

4. Equity financing involves sharing:

(A) Profitability

(B) Risk

5. Which financing option may lead to dilution of ownership and control?

(A) Debt

(B) Equity

6. Debt financing comes with the risk of:

(A) Legal action

(B) Loss of expertise

7. Which financing option may provide access to industry knowledge and networks?

(A) Debt

(B) Equity

8. Equity investors share in the:

(A) Success or failure of the business

(B) Repayment obligation of the business

9. Debt financing involves:

(A) Fixed interest payments

(B) No interest payments

10. Which financing option allows for potential greater funding?

(A) Debt

(B) Equity

For the answers to this and the other quizzes, visit MoneyMasterHQ.com/Books.

Chapter Takeaway

Understanding investments, debt, and equity is critical for businesses looking for financial resources and opportunities for growth. Investments enable the strategic allocation of capital, generate potential returns, and expand operations. Debt financing provides benefits such as tax deductions and retained ownership, but it also carries the risks of repayment obligations and potential legal action. On the other hand, equity financing allows for shared risk and access to expertise but may result in dilution of ownership and control.

Businesses can make informed decisions to optimize their capital structure and pursue sustainable growth by carefully weighing the pros and cons of each option. To achieve financial stability, support business goals, and ensure long-term success, it is critical to balance investments, debt, and equity.

Segue to Next Chapter

Running a successful and profitable business necessitates a blend of strategic thinking, operational efficiency, and sound decision-making. In the following chapter, we will review the key topics covered in previous chapters, such as understanding financial statements, budgeting, and cash flows. We will explain why these are critical concepts for a non-financial manager to understand.

Chapter 13:

The Business Success Blueprint

Using Finance and Accounting

Welcome to the final chapter of this book, which I am confident will prove to be immensely valuable if put into practice. Managers who are not part of the finance department can significantly benefit from understanding the essentials of accounting and finance. This knowledge empowers them to effectively interpret their company's financial data and make informed decisions that contribute to the organization's overall success.

Assessing the Accounting and Finance Function

Begin by evaluating whether your company's accounting and finance functions are maintaining financial records accurately and efficiently. Review the processes in place for recording transactions, reconciling accounts, and preparing financial statements. Identify any gaps or discrepancies that may indicate issues with the accuracy or timeliness of financial reporting. If necessary, implement measures to improve the accounting function, such as hiring additional staff, investing in better accounting software, or providing training to existing team members.

Key Financial Concepts and Terminology

Once you're confident in the quality of your company's financial records, familiarize yourself with the essential financial terms and concepts that are crucial for making sound business decisions. This was discussed in detail in Chapter 3.

Some key terms that we discussed in this book include:

- **Balance sheet:** A snapshot of a company's assets, liabilities, and equity at a specific point in time.

- **Income statement:** A report that shows a company's revenue, expenses, and net income over a period of time.

- **Cash flow statement:** A summary of a company's cash inflows and outflows during a specific period, categorized into operating, investing, and financing activities.

- **Budget:** A financial plan that outlines expected revenue and expenses for a particular period.

Now take a look at the double-entry system that we discussed, consider 10 of the most common transactions that take place in the business, and check how they are being recorded. Are you able to identify which accounts each of these types of transactions affects?

Take a look at some of the principles we discussed in this book, such as the matching principle. See if this is applied in the financial statements. For example, in a given month, check if the revenues and all related expenses to achieve that revenue have been correctly reported. If not, check with the Finance and Accounting team as to how this could be rectified.

Understanding Financial Statements

Evaluate your company's financial health by understanding the main components of financial statements and how to interpret them effectively. This concept was discussed in detail in Chapter 4.

Analyze balance sheets, income statements, and cash flow statements to assess profitability, liquidity, and financial stability. Make it a habit to review these statements regularly, identifying areas that require attention or improvement. Calculate the cash conversion cycle of the business. How has it been moving over the past few periods (e.g., month-on-month change over the past six months, compared with the same time last year, and so on)?

Financial Ratios and Performance Metrics

Ratios were discussed in detail in Chapter 6.

Track key financial values, ratios, and performance metrics to assess your company's financial health and make informed decisions.

- Revenue, gross profit, expenses, operating profit, EBITDA, profit before tax, and profit after tax values from the income statement. Monitor these numbers periodically, check how they compare with prior periods? Is there a trend and what is it? Is there anything that can be done to improve the business performance? Any new customer segments? New markets?

- The cash flow movements for the period under the main three categories of operating, investing, and financing cash flows. How do they compare with the previous periods? Is there a trend and what is it? How can the cash flows be improved?

- Liquidity ratios (e.g., current ratio, quick ratio) measure your company's ability to meet short-term obligations.

- Profitability ratios (e.g., gross profit margin, net profit margin, return on equity) evaluate your company's earnings relative to its revenue, assets, or equity.

- Solvency ratios (e.g., debt-to-equity ratio, equity ratio) assess your company's ability to meet long-term obligations and its financial stability.

Regularly monitor these ratios, comparing them against industry benchmarks and your company's historical performance.

Budgeting and Cash Flow Management

Please see Chapter 9 for a detailed explanation.

Create and maintain budgets for ensuring financial stability.

- Does the company have budgets prepared? If not, initiate discussions with the respective teams and develop a budget based on historical data, future projections, and strategic goals. Review it regularly to track progress and make adjustments as needed.

- After each month, check for variances (variance analysis, which was discussed in the book in Chapter 5).

- Aside from an overall budget, are there any specific budgets that could be important to the company?

- Implement cash flow management strategies to optimize working capital and maintain liquidity.

For example, negotiating extended credit terms with vendors and checking if any credit provided to customers could be reduced. Monitor cash inflows and outflows, identifying ways to increase cash reserves and minimize cash shortages, if any. See if the cash flow forecast is updated for the upcoming month on a regular basis.

Cost Control and Expense Analysis

Control costs and analyze expenses for business growth.

- Review the top expense lines (for example, top 10 expenses) in your income statement, identifying cost saving opportunities and areas for improvement.

- Implement cost control measures, such as renegotiating contracts, streamlining processes, or investing in more efficient technology, to enhance operational efficiency and profitability.

Evaluate the expense patterns and analyze the fixed versus variable expenses as well as how they have been moving over the last three periods.

Debt and Equity Financing

Understand the role of debt and equity financing in your company's capital structure. For a detailed discussion, see Chapter 11.

Evaluate your company's current capital structure and determine the optimal mix of debt and equity financing.

Regularly reassess your financing strategy to account for changes in market conditions, interest rates, and your company's financial performance.

Investment Evaluation Techniques

Check what methods are currently used to evaluate investment projects in the business. Use methods like payback period, net present value (NPV), and internal rate of return (IRR) to evaluate long-term investment projects.

- **Payback period:** Calculate the time it takes for an investment to generate enough cash flow to recover its initial cost.

- **NPV:** Find the present value of future cash flows that an investment will generate, discounted by the required rate of return. A positive NPV indicates a profitable investment.

- **IRR:** Calculate the discount rate at which an investment's NPV equals zero. Compare the IRR to your required rate of return to assess an investment's viability.

How can decision-making be improved on investment evaluations? What measures are in place to continuously monitor their performance against the expected outcomes?

Internal Controls, Compliance, and External Audits

Establishing internal controls is crucial for accurate financial reporting and fraud prevention.

- Implement control measures, such as segregation of duties, authorization procedures, and regular audits, to maintain the integrity of your financial data.

- Ensure compliance with relevant laws and regulations, such as tax laws, industry-specific regulations, and accounting standards, to avoid penalties and safeguard your company's reputation.

Check if all compliance-related requirements have been met in the recent past. What are the upcoming requirements (e.g., tax return to be submitted in the upcoming month)?

Are the financials of the business audited at least annually? If not, check how it can be audited. Compare costs from different audit firms, sign a Non-Disclosure Agreement, and look to have the financials externally and independently audited for peace of mind. Check the findings that the external, independent auditors have provided and take any necessary and appropriate corrective actions.

Management Accounting

Utilize management accounting techniques to support decision-making and improve operational efficiency. Management accounting is discussed in Chapter 10 in detail.

- Implement activity-based costing to allocate indirect costs more accurately and identify cost drivers.

- Use variance analysis to compare actual performance against budgeted performance and identify areas for improvement.

- Conduct a break-even analysis to determine the level of sales needed to cover all costs and inform pricing strategies.

- Apply forecasting techniques, such as trend and regression analysis, to predict future financial performance and inform strategic planning.

Continuing Education and Skill Development

Invest in ongoing financial education and skill development to stay updated on best practices and industry trends.

Attend workshops, webinars, or courses to enhance your financial knowledge and skills and stay informed about changes in financial regulations, accounting standards, and market conditions.

Financial excellence is not a destination but an ongoing journey of continuous improvement. By consistently implementing these strategies and insights, non-finance managers and business owners can not only elevate their company's financial performance but also empower themselves to make informed decisions that drive the overall success of their organization. In the pursuit of excellence, knowledge and measurement become the keys to unlocking your business' true potential.

Chapter Takeaway

In this chapter, we have explored the essential elements of running a successful business from the perspective of non-financial managers. By understanding the key principles and practices discussed throughout this chapter, you are equipped with valuable insights to drive business success.

By understanding and implementing the key concepts covered in this chapter, you will be able to develop a clear picture of your business' financial health and align your goals with the overall strategic direction. By gaining a basic understanding of financial statements, budgets, and cash flow management. You will also be able to create a comprehensive marketing strategy as you will be able to do a detailed evaluation of your target market, pricing strategy, and where you can expand on your offering.

Remember, running a successful business requires a multidimensional approach that balances financial acumen, strategic thinking, and a customer-centric mindset. With the knowledge you have gained from this chapter, you will be empowered to make data-driven and informed decisions, as well as steer your organization toward long-term success.

Conclusion

Congratulations! You have completed the transformative journey through Accounting Fundamentals: A Non-Finance Manager's Guide to Finance and Accounting.

We have explored the realm of accounting and its significance in the world of business during our journey through *Accounting Fundamentals: A Non-Finance Manager's Guide to Finance and Accounting*. We set out on this educational journey with the intention of empowering non-financial managers with the expertise they need to make sense of the intricate worlds of finance and accounting. As we come to the end of this book, consider the significance of accounting and how it intersects with management principles.

Accounting, at its core, is the language of business. It provides a structured framework for recording, analyzing, and communicating financial information, serving as a compass to guide decision-making processes. By embracing accounting fundamentals, non-financial managers gain a deeper understanding of their organization's financial health and performance, allowing them to contribute effectively to strategic planning and operational decision-making.

One vital aspect of accounting that we explored in detail is management accounting. This branch of accounting focuses on generating timely and relevant financial information for internal use within an organization. It goes beyond the traditional financial statements to provide insights into cost analysis, budgeting, performance measurement, and forecasting. By applying management accounting principles, non-financial managers can monitor key performance indicators, evaluate project profitability, identify cost-saving opportunities, and optimize resource allocation.

Through our exploration of various accounting concepts and principles, we have uncovered the significance of accuracy, transparency, and ethical practices in financial reporting. Accounting plays a pivotal role in ensuring compliance with legal and regulatory requirements, promoting accountability, and building trust with stakeholders. By upholding these principles, non-financial managers contribute to the overall financial integrity and sustainability of their organization.

In conclusion, *Accounting Fundamentals: A Non Finance Manager's Guide to Finance and Accounting* empowers non-financial managers with the knowledge and tools to navigate the dynamic world of finance and accounting. By embracing accounting principles, non-financial managers can speak the language of business, make informed decisions, and contribute to the success of their organization. Remember, accounting is not just a task for the finance department, but an essential tool for all managers seeking to drive growth, enhance profitability, and ensure long-term success.

As you embark on your journey beyond these pages, may you continue to embrace the power of accounting, apply management accounting principles, and unleash your full potential as a non-financial manager. The world of finance and accounting awaits, and with your newfound knowledge, you are equipped to navigate it with confidence and finesse. Here's to your continued success!

Index

References

Accounting Tools. (2023, July 8). *Financial analysis*. AccountingTools. https://www.accountingtools.com/articles/what-is-financial-analysis.html

Accounting Tools. (2023, March 21). *Labor variance*. AccountingTools. https://www.accountingtools.com/articles/what-is-a-labor-variance.html

ADP. (2021, July 9). *What are payroll deductions? Pre-tax & post-tax deductions*. ADP. https://www.adp.com/resources/articles-and-insights/articles/p/payroll-deductions.aspx

BDC. (2023). *What are retained earnings?* BDC. https://www.bdc.ca/en/articles-tools/entrepreneur-toolkit/templates-business-guides/glossary/retained-earnings#:~:text=Retained%20earnings%20are%20the%20amount

Berry, T. (2023, March 17). *How to create an expense budget*. Bplans. https://www.bplans.com/business-planning/how-to-write/financial-plan/expense-budget

Bragg, S. (2023, April 11). *Equity definition*. AccountingTools. https://www.accountingtools.com/articles/equity-1

Case, J. (2023, May 26). *From survival to growth: Leveraging the power of financial management systems*. Forbes. https://www.forbes.com/sites/forbestechcouncil/2023/05/26/from-survival-to-growth-leveraging-the-power-of-financial-management-systems/?sh=4ba22c607db2

CFI. (2023, April 20). *Types of Financial Analysis.* Corporate Finance Institute. https://corporatefinanceinstitute.com/resources/accounting/types-of-financial-analysis

Chambers, J., Mullick, S., & Smith, D. (2019, August). *How to choose the right forecasting technique.* Harvard Business Review. https://hbr.org/1971/07/how-to-choose-the-right-forecasting-technique

DT Finance. (2023, April 27). *Importance of management accounting, strategies, and customer satisfaction.* Datatrained.com. https://datatrained.com/dt-finance/importance-of-management-accounting/#:~:text=The%20Importance%20of%20management%20accounting%20is%20to%20enhance%20managerial%20performance

Dunn, P. E. (2020, April 15). *Capital investment appraisal explained.* PQ Magazine. https://www.pqmagazine.com/capital-investment-appraisal-explained/

FindLaw. (2019, July 23). *Debt vs. equity -- advantages and disadvantages.* Findlaw. https://www.findlaw.com/smallbusiness/business-finances/debt-vs-equity-advantages-and-disadvantages.html#:~:text=%22Debt%22%20involves%20borrowing%20money%20to

Goodreads. (2023). *A quote by Anthony Robbins.* Goodreads. https://www.goodreads.com/quotes/877199-the-only-impossible-journey-is-the-one-you-never-begin

Henn, P. (2023). *What is net profit, definition and meaning?* Capital. https://capital.com/net-profit-definition

Hodge, S. (2022, August 23). *The compliance costs of IRS regulations* Tax Foundation. https://taxfoundation.org/tax-compliance-costs-irs-regulations

Holtzman, M. P. (2022, February 22). *Managerial accounting for dummies cheat sheet.* Dummies. https://www.dummies.com/article/business-careers-money/business/accounting/general-accounting/managerial-accounting-for-dummies-cheat-sheet-208085

IEduNote. (2018, June 20). *History and evolution of accounting.* IEduNote. https://www.iedunote.com/accounting-evolution-history

Indeed. (2023, February 3). *Guide to creating a business forecast (with examples).* Indeed. https://www.indeed.com/career-advice/career-development/business-forecast#:~:text=A%20business%20forecast%20provides%20companies,investments%20or%20seeking%20outside%20funding.

IRS. (2023). *Understanding taxes - theme 4: What is taxed and why, direct and indirect taxes.* Internal Revenue Service. https://apps.irs.gov/app/understandingTaxes/teacher/whys_thm04_les04.jsp#:~:text=A%20direct%20tax%20is%20one

Janeczko, B. (2023, April 13). *Business plan 101: Sales & marketing.* Score. https://www.score.org/resource/blog-post/business-plan-101-sales-marketing

Kagan, J. (2019). *Direct tax.* Investopedia. https://www.investopedia.com/terms/d/directtax.asp

Kagan, J. (2022, April 4). *What is an indirect tax?* Investopedia. https://www.investopedia.com/terms/i/indirecttax.asp

Kelwig, D. (2021, November 9). *What is a sales budget? Use, example, and purpose.* Zendesk. https://www.zendesk.com/blog/sales-budget/#:~:text=A%20sales%20budget%20is%20a

Kenton, W. (2021, November 17). *Variable overhead efficiency variance.* Investopedia. https://www.investopedia.com/terms/v/variable-overhead-efficiency-variance.asp

Kimatu, E. (2023, February 4). *Depreciation vs. amortization: definitions, differences, and examples.* Indeed. https://www.indeed.com/career-advice/career-development/depreciation-vs-amortization

Krishnan, V. (2019, September 2). *Managerial accounting - definition, objectives, and techniques.* Essential Business Guides. https://www.zoho.com/books/guides/management-accounting.html#:~:text=What%20is%20management%20accounting%3F

Krishnan, V. (2020, July 3). *Business budget 101: importance, components, and types.* Essential Business Guides. https://www.zoho.com/books/guides/basics-of-business-budgets.html

Lavinsky, D. (2018). *The business planning process: 5 steps to creating a new plan.* Growthink. https://www.growthink.com/businessplan/help-center/business-planning-process-5-steps-creating-new-plan

Leonard, K., & Watts, R. (2021, November 29). *The ultimate guide To S.M.A.R.T. goals.* Forbes. https://www.forbes.com/advisor/business/smart-goals/

Maheshwari, R. (2022, October 12). Difference between direct and indirect taxes. Forbes.

https://www.forbes.com/advisor/in/tax/difference-between-direct-and-indirect-tax

Maheshwari, R. (2022, October 12). *Difference between direct and indirect taxes.* Forbes. https://www.forbes.com/advisor/in/tax/difference-between-direct-and-indirect-tax/

Maryville University. (2022, October 4). *History of Accounting: How It's Evolved Over Time.* Maryville Online. https://online.maryville.edu/blog/history-of-accounting/

Medleva, V. (2023). *Investment fund: meaning and definition* Capital. https://capital.com/investment-fund-definition

Miller, T. (2019, April 22). *History of accounting: Timeline.* TheStreet. https://www.thestreet.com/investing/history-of-accounting-timeline-14944095

Mohitg539. (2022, September 11). *Reserves and their types.* GeeksforGeeks. https://www.geeksforgeeks.org/reserves-and-its-types/

Neumark, F., McLure, C. E., & Cox, M. S. (2023, June 1). *Taxation - policy, collection, reform, and systems.* Britannica. https://www.britannica.com/money/topic/taxation/History-of-taxation

Nicastro, S., & Murphy, R. (2022, July 26). *How to write a business plan, step by step.* NerdWallet. https://www.nerdwallet.com/article/small-business/business-plan

O'Shea, A., Lam-Balfour, T., & Durana, A. (2022, November 21). *What is a dividend?* NerdWallet. https://www.nerdwallet.com/article/investing/what-are-dividends

Parrot, W. (2023). *Advanced investment appraisal.* ACCA Global. https://www.accaglobal.com/gb/en/student/exam-support-resources/fundamentals-exams-study-resources/f9/technical-articles/advanced-investment-appraisal.html#:~:text=The%20methods%20of%20investment%20appraisal

PaySimple. (2018, April 3). *Common accounting terms and acronyms business owners should know.* PaySimple. https://paysimple.com/blog/42-basic-accounting-terms-you-should-know

PWC. (2023). *Tax compliance services.* PricewaterhouseCoopers. https://www.pwc.com/us/en/services/tax/tax-compliance-services.html

Quote by Helen Keller. (2019). BrainyQuote. https://www.brainyquote.com/quotes/helen_keller_382259

Quote by Warren Buffet. (2012, October 15). *Best Warren Buffett Quotes,* by Topic. 25iq. https://25iq.com/quotations/warren-buffett/#:~:text=Accounting%3A

Quote Master. (2023). *Quote by Charlie Munger.* Quote Master. https://www.quotemaster.org/q91b2340de8d77363b392b5fe4 2d5ae71

Rotich, R. (2023, February 4). 7 *Types of financial analysis (with definition and examples).* Indeed. https://www.indeed.com/career-advice/career-development/financial-analysis-definition-and-examples

Russo, K. (2022, May 19). *Break-even point explained.* Oracle NetSuite. https://www.netsuite.com/portal/resource/articles/accounting/break-even-point-bep.shtml

SBA. (2023). *Break-Even Point*. U.S. Small Business Administration. https://www.sba.gov/breakevenpointcalculator#:~:text=The %20break%2Deven%20point%20is

Schmidt, J. (2023, April 21). *Operating budget*. Corporate Finance Institute. https://corporatefinanceinstitute.com/resources/fpa/operatin g-budget/

Schwarz, L. (2022, June 7). *Performing a cash flow check-up*. Oracle NetSuite. https://www.netsuite.com/portal/resource/articles/financial-management/cash-flow-analysis.shtml

Srivastav, A. K. (2020, March 31). *Limitations of financial accounting*. WallStreetMojo. https://www.wallstreetmojo.com/limitations-of-financial-accounting/#:~:text=Financial%20Accounting%20does%20no t%20provide

Take-Profit. (2023). *United States corporate tax rate 2023*. Take-Profit. https://take-profit.org/en/statistics/corporate-tax-rate/united-states/#:~:text=Corporate%20Tax%20Rate%20in%20United %20States%20remained%20unchanged%20at%2021

Tamplin, T. (2023a, March 9). *Direct Labor variances formula, types, calculation, examples*. Finance Strategist. https://www.financestrategists.com/accounting/variance-analysis/direct-labor-variances/

Tamplin, T. (2023b, March 29). *What Is EBITDA? History, formula, benefits, and drawbacks*. Finance Strategist. https://www.financestrategists.com/wealth-management/financial-statements/ebitda/?gclid=CjwKCAjw1YCkBhAOEiwA5aN4A U1wV0lrLa940EQnwQ22NH3H-GF7-cgUMMa7cR1UzOrlfxtlNCaFRBoC8rgQAvD_BwE

Tamplin, T. (2023c, April 11). *How to compute various overhead cost variances formulas.* Finance Strategist. https://www.financestrategists.com/accounting/management-accounting/compute-various-overhead-cost-variances/

Tamplin, T. (2023d, May 2). *Material variances, formula, calculation, examples, and FAQs.* Finance Strategist. https://www.financestrategists.com/accounting/variance-analysis/material-variances/?gclid=CjwKCAjwsvujBhAXEiwA_UXnAOWvV1_2H2IN6HODzZjwjB68qzg7G2MZFRplBjcS2n0FQCiG6RmnMxoCC7sQAvD_BwE

Tax Policy Center. (2023). *How do taxes affect the economy in the long run?* Tax Policy Center. https://www.taxpolicycenter.org/briefing-book/how-do-taxes-affect-economy-long-run#:~:text=By%20influencing%20incentives%2C%20taxes%20can

The Business Research Company. (2022, June). *Global Accounting Services Market Data and Industry Research Analysis.* The Business Research Company. https://www.thebusinessresearchcompany.com/report/accounting-services-market

WallStreetPrep. (2023). *Other comprehensive income (OCI).* Wall Street Prep. https://www.wallstreetprep.com/knowledge/oci-other-comprehensive-income/

Image References

Alexander Grey. (2019, July 4). *Pile of mail waiting to be sorted.* Unsplash. https://unsplash.com/photos/tn57JI3CewI

Barbhuiya, T. (2021, October 2). *A person stacking coins.* Unsplash. https://unsplash.com/photos/jpqyfK7GB4w

Boran, I. (2021, May 28). *100 Euro and 100 Dollar banknotes.* Unsplash. https://unsplash.com/photos/T_PothPoL-g

Chisu, R. (2018, April 9). *Low angle photography of man.* Unsplash. https://unsplash.com/photos/Ua-agENjmI4

Chong, N. (2020, May 24). *Bitcoin price chart from trading view.* Unsplash. https://unsplash.com/photos/N__BnvQ_w18

Distel, A. (2019, June 3). *Equity.* Unsplash. https://unsplash.com/photos/goFBjlQiZFU

Ds_30. (2020, March 4). *Diagrams, graphs, charts image.* Pixabay. https://pixabay.com/photos/diagrams-graphs-charts-trading-4900983/

Firmbee. (2015, June 18). *Person holding white Samsung.* Unsplash. https://unsplash.com/photos/jrh5lAq-mIs

Geralt. (2017, November 6). *Success curve arrow.* Pixabay. https://pixabay.com/photos/success-curve-arrow-turn-on-2917048/

Hall, N. (2021, February 13). *Woman in a white long sleeve shirt.* Unsplash. https://unsplash.com/photos/o8KUqjk9gqE

Mohamed_hassan. (2018, March 13). *Teamwork, brainstorm.* Pixabay. https://pixabay.com/photos/teamwork-cooperation-brainstorming-3213924/

Nattanan23. (2017, September 6). *Keyboard image.* Pixabay. https://pixabay.com/photos/hand-type-keyboard-money-finance-2722098/

PublicDomainPictures. (2012, February 28). *Coins, money, profit*. Pixabay. https://pixabay.com/photos/coins-money-profit-savings-stack-18134/

Sikkema, K. (2019, April 2). *Black Android smartphone near a tax form*. Unsplash. https://unsplash.com/photos/M98NRBuzbpc

Stevepb. (2015, November 17). *Calculator*. Pixabay. https://pixabay.com/photos/calculator-calculation-insurance-1044173/

Stevepb. (2017, September 27). *Savings_budget_investment_money*. Pixabay. https://pixabay.com/photos/savings-budget-investment-money-2789112/

Succo. (2014, October 13). *Abacus*. Pixabay. https://pixabay.com/photos/abacus-calculate-mathematics-485704/

Tumisu. (2018, April 5). *Analytics graph chart*. Pixabay. https://pixabay.com/photos/analytics-graph-chart-data-3291738/

Tumisu. (2020, February 6). *Chart, investment, analytics*. Pixabay. https://pixabay.com/photos/chart-investment-analytics-graph-4819676/

Winkler, M. (2020, June 9). *Black and silver laptop*. Unsplash. https://unsplash.com/photos/IrRbSND5EUc